Heroes of
the Civil War

Heroes of
the Civil War

HARRISON HUNT

MILITARY PRESS
New York

This 1990 edition was published by Military Press, a division of dilithium Press, Ltd., distributed by Crown Publishers Inc., a Random House Company, 225 Park Avenue South, New York, New York 10003

8 7 6 5 4 3 2 1

ISBN   0 517 01739 3

Printed and bound in Hong Kong

Heroes of the Civil War was prepared and produced by M & M Books, 11 W. 19th Street, New York, New York 10011

AN M & M BOOK

Project Director & Editor Gary Fishgall

Senior Editorial Assistant Shirley Vierheller
Editorial Assistants Ben McLaughlin, Maxine Dormer, Ben D'Amprisi, Jr. **Copy Editor** Bert N. Zelman of Publishers Workshop Inc.

Photo Research Maxine Dormer, Harrison Hunt, Lucinda Stellini

Designer Binns & Lubin/Martin Lubin

Separations and Printing Regent Publishing Services Ltd.

(preceding pages) The Battle of Petersburg, Virginia, on April 2, 1865, as seen in a print by Currier & Ives.

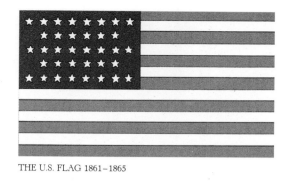

THE U.S. FLAG 1861–1865

CONTENTS

THE CONFEDERATE BATTLE AND NAVY FLAG

Introduction

No event in American history inspired greater devotion to ideals or sparked nobler acts of heroism than did the Civil War. More than 4 million American fighting men, supported by millions more on the home front, risked their lives to either preserve one nation, the United States, or create a new one, the Confederate States. *Heroes of the Civil War* tells the story, in words and pictures, of 70 of the men and women who did the most to aid their causes during the War Between the States.

Selecting the 35 Confederate and 35 Union figures profiled in *Heroes* was no easy task. Dozens of noteworthy men and women could have qualified. Ultimately, the choice was determined on the basis of wartime accomplishment: achievements above and beyond the ordinary, on or off the battlefield. Outstanding leaders such as Lee and Grant have naturally been included, but some famous generals like Ambrose Burnside and Braxton Bragg have not because they did not measure up as effective commanders. A few others—Daniel Sickles and George Pickett, for example—are clearly controversial; read-ers can form their own opinions as to the merits of including them among the greats.

While *Heroes of the Civil War* concentrates on the generals and admirals who led the Union and Confederate war efforts, it is not limited to the most well-known commanders. This book also includes a number of unsung heroes and heroines whose stories may be new even to the most avid Civil War buffs—people like Josiah Gorgas, the creative head of the Confederate Ordnance Department; Elizabeth Van Lew, Union spy in Richmond; Stand Watie, the South's Cherokee general; 74-year-old John Burns, the only civilian to fight at Gettysburg; Sally Tompkins, the only woman to receive an officer's commission from the Confederate Army; and Martin Delany, the highest-ranking African-American in the Union Army. My only regret is that the scope of the book did not permit me to include a section on the real heroes of the war: the millions of plain soldiers and sea-men, North and South, who left their homes and loved ones to fight for the causes they believed in. To them, more than any commander, belongs the honor and the glory.

Even more difficult than selecting the subjects was encapsulating their lives in the relatively short essays you will find in this volume. The profiles, therefore, concentrate on wartime service and skip over many details of these fascinating peoples' peacetime lives. Virtually every one of them is the subject of at least one booklength biography, so if this collection piques your interest in some of these heroic men and women, as I hope it will, you can easily find out more about them.

The illustrations reproduced here include period photographs, paintings, drawings, and prints as well as appropriate photos of battlefields as they appear now. All of the images have been carefully selected to capture the personalities of the people profiled and the spirit of the war in which they served. The pictures and the colorful stories accompanying them combine to make *Heroes of the Civil War* a book for casual readers and Civil War enthusiasts alike.

(opposite) *This display honors Ephraim Ellsworth, the first Union officer to die in the Civil War (see p. 94).*

Civil War Chronology

1860

Nov. 6	Abraham Lincoln elected President of the United States; Hannibal Hamlin, Vice-President
Dec. 20	South Carolina secedes
Dec. 26	Maj. Robert Anderson moves U.S. garrison in Charleston, South Carolina, to Fort Sumter

1861

Jan. 9	Union ship *Star of the West* fired upon while attempting to reinforce Fort Sumter; Mississippi secedes
Jan. 10	Florida secedes
Jan. 11	Alabama secedes
Jan. 19	Georgia secedes
Jan. 26	Louisiana secedes
Feb. 1	Texas secedes
Feb. 8	Constitution of the Confederate States of America adopted
Feb. 9	Jefferson Davis elected provisional President of the Confederacy; Alexander Stephens, Vice-President
Feb. 18	Davis and Stephens inaugurated
March 4	Lincoln and Hamlin inaugurated
April 12	Fort Sumter fired upon
April 14	Fort Sumter surrenders
April 15	President Lincoln, declaring a state of war, calls for 75,000 soldiers to put down insurrection
April 17	Virginia secedes
May 6	Arkansas secedes
May 20	North Carolina secedes
June 8	Tennessee secedes
July 21	First Battle of Bull Run (or Manassas), Virginia
Aug. 10	Battle of Wilson's Creek, Missouri
Nov. 1	George B. McClellan appointed general-in-chief of U.S. Army

1862

Feb. 16	Confederate Fort Donelson, Tennessee, "unconditionally surrenders" to Gen. U. S. Grant
March–June	Stonewall Jackson's Shenandoah Valley campaign
March 7–8	Battle of Pea Ridge, Arkansas
March 9	Naval engagement between U.S.S. *Monitor* and C.S.S. *Virginia* (formerly *Merrimack*)
March 11	George B. McClellan removed as head of Union armies; kept as commander of the Army of the Potomac
March 17	Federal Army of the Potomac begins Peninsular campaign in Virginia
April 6–7	Battle of Shiloh, Tennessee
April 25	Flag officer David Farragut captures New Orleans, Louisiana
May 25	First Battle of Winchester, Virginia
May 31	Battle of Fair Oaks, Virginia
June 1	Robert E. Lee named commander of Confederate Army in Virginia
June 25– July 1	Seven Days' Battles on Virginia Peninsula:
June 25	Battle of Oak Grove
June 26	Battle of Mechanicsville, or Beaver Dam Creek
June 27	Battle of Gaines' Mill
June 29	Battle of Savage's Station
June 30	Battle of White Oak Swamp
July 1	Battle of Malvern Hill
July 11	Henry Halleck named new general-in-chief of U.S. Army
Aug. 9	Battle of Cedar Mountain, Virginia
Aug. 28	Battle of Groveton, Virginia
Aug. 29–30	Second Battle of Bull Run, Virginia
Sept. 1	Battle of Chantilly, Virginia
Sept. 14	Battle of South Mountain, Maryland
Sept. 15	Harpers Ferry captured by Stonewall Jackson
Sept. 17	Battle of Antietam, Maryland
Sept. 22	President Lincoln issues Emancipation Proclamation
Oct. 3–4	Battle of Corinth, Mississippi
Oct. 8	Battle of Perryville, Kentucky
Nov. 5	Ambrose Burnside replaces George B. McClellan as commander of the Army of the Potomac
Nov. 24	Joseph E. Johnston appointed commander of Confederate forces west of the Alleghenies
Dec. 13	Battle of Fredericksburg, Virginia

THE BATTLE OF SHILOH, TENNESSEE

CONFEDERATE TROOPS CROSSING THE POTOMAC

1863

Dec. 31–Jan. 2	Battle of Stones River, Tennessee
Jan. 1	Emancipation Proclamation goes into effect in areas under rebellion
Jan. 25	Joseph Hooker replaces Ambrose Burnside as commander of the Army of the Potomac
March 3	Draft enacted by U.S. government
April 16	U.S. Adm. David Porter's ships pass Confederate artillery batteries overlooking the Mississippi River at Vicksburg
May 1–4	Battle of Chancellorsville, Virginia
May 18	Union siege of Vicksburg, Mississippi, begins
June 9	Battle of Brandy Station, Virginia
June 13–15	Second Battle of Winchester, Virginia
June 28	George G. Meade replaces Joseph Hooker as commander of the Army of the Potomac
July	John H. Morgan's raid into Ohio and Indiana
July 1–3	Battle of Gettysburg, Pennsylvania
July 4	Vicksburg, Mississippi, surrenders to Gen. U. S. Grant
Sept. 9	Chattanooga captured by Union forces
Sept. 19–20	Battle of Chickamauga, Georgia
Oct. 16	Ulysses S. Grant given command of Western armies of the United States
Nov. 19	Lincoln delivers his Gettysburg Address at the dedication of the National Cemetery there
Nov. 23–25	Battle of Chattanooga, Tennessee

1864

March 9	Ulysses S. Grant named general-in-chief of all U.S. armies
May 5–6	Battle of the Wilderness, Virginia
May 8–19	Battle of Spotsylvania Court House, Virginia
May 11	Battle of Yellow Tavern, Virginia
May 13–15	Battle of Resaca, Georgia
June 1–3	Battle of Cold Harbor, Virginia
June 18	Union siege of Petersburg, Virginia begins
June 19	C.S.S. *Alabama* sunk by U.S.S. *Kearsarge*
June 27	Battle of Kennesaw Mountain, Georgia
June 27–Aug. 7	Gen. Jubal Early's Raid on Washington, D.C.
July 9	Battle of Monocacy, Maryland
July 22	Battle of Atlanta, Georgia
Aug. 23	Mobile Bay, Alabama, captured by Adm. David G. Farragut
Aug. 29	Democratic party nominates George B. McClellan for President of the United States
Sept. 2	Atlanta, Georgia, occupied by U.S. forces
Sept. 19	Third Battle of Winchester, Virginia
Oct. 19	Battle of Cedar Creek, Virginia
Nov. 8	Abraham Lincoln reelected President of the United States Andrew Johnson, Vice-President
Nov. 16	General Sherman begins his "March to the Sea"
Nov. 30	Battle of Franklin, Tennessee

Dec. 15–16	Battle of Nashville, Tennessee
Dec. 20	Confederate forces evacuate Savannah, Georgia

1865

Jan. 31	Robert E. Lee appointed general-in-chief of Confederate Armies
Feb. 1	Gen. William T. Sherman begins his Carolina campaign
Feb. 17	Columbia and Charleston, South Carolina, fall to U.S. forces
March 4	Abraham Lincoln inaugurated for second term as President
April 1	Battle of Five Forks, Virginia
April 2	Richmond and Petersburg, Virginia, abandoned by Confederate forces; Jefferson Davis and the Confederate government flee the capital

GEN. PHILIP SHERIDAN

April 6	Battle of Sayler's Creek, Virginia
April 9	General Lee surrenders Army of Northern Virginia to General Grant at Appomattox Court House, Virginia
April 13	General Sherman captures Raleigh, North Carolina
April 14	President Lincoln assassinated by John Wilkes Booth
April 15	Lincoln dies; Andrew Johnson sworn in as President
April 26	Gen. Joseph E. Johnston surrenders the Confederate troops in North Carolina to General Sherman; John Wilkes Booth killed
May 10	Jefferson Davis captured at Irwinville, Georgia
May 26	Confederate forces west of the Mississippi River surrender, ending the war

The Union

Robert Anderson 1805 – 1871

★ ★ ★ ★ ★ ★ ★ ★ ★ ★ ★ ★ ★

It is particularly appropriate for this volume to begin with Robert Anderson, for he commanded the beleaguered Union garrison at Fort Sumter that felt the first shots of the War Between the States. After his stand in Charleston harbor, Anderson became a hero throughout the North, and when he raised the flag over the conquered fort four years later he symbolized victory for the entire United States.

Anderson was born near Lexington, Kentucky, on June 14, 1805, the son of Richard Anderson, Sr., a former lieutenant-colonel in the Continental Army. Inspired by his father, Robert entered West Point in 1821 and upon graduation in 1825 was commissioned a lieutenant in the 3rd U.S. Artillery. After serving in the Black Hawk and Seminole Wars and as an assistant adjutant-general, Anderson was promoted to captain and posted to Gen. Winfield Scott's command in the Mexican War. At the close of that conflict, Anderson was assigned to administrative duties, including teaching artillery tactics at West Point, and was promoted to major in 1857.

As the agitation for secession was reaching a peak in South Carolina in November 1860, Major Anderson was given the unenviable command of the Federal defenses at Charleston. The Buchanan administration believed that Anderson, a proslavery Southerner married to a Georgian, would be a less controversial commander than the Northerner previously assigned there. However, Anderson made it clear to the Carolinians that, what-

Maj. Robert Anderson, the Union officer whose determined stand at Fort Sumter brought the country to civil war.

(previous pages) **Grant and His Generals** *is a composite 1865 painting by Ole Peter Hansen Balling.* **It shows Grant with many of the Union's heroes of the Civil War, including Philip Sheridan, James McPherson, George Thomas, George Meade, and William T. Sherman.**

An artist's conception of the interior of Fort Sumter during the bombardment.

On April 14, 1865, four years to the day after he struck the American flag at Sumter, Anderson returned to the recaptured fort to raise the Stars and Stripes once again.

personal views, his duty was to the States and he would not turn over any property under his control without orders from Washington, D.C.

Anderson's garrison was stationed at Fort Moultrie, a 50-year-old fortification on the eastern entrance to Charleston harbor. The major realized that Moultrie was indefensible and that Fort Sumter, located on an island in the center of the harbor, provided much better protection. But he had no authorization to move his troops there. After South Carolina seceded on December 20, Anderson finally received permission from the War Department to relocate. On the night of December 26, his command secretly abandoned Moultrie and rowed out to Sumter.

Anderson and his 127 men remained isolated on Sumter for more than three months, slowly running out of supplies while Confederate forces under Gen. P.G.T. Beauregard prepared artillery emplacements against them. On April 10, 1861, as Federal ships were steaming toward Sumter to resupply the Yankees, Beauregard demanded the fort's surrender. Anderson refused, and at 4:30 A.M. on April 12 the first shots of the bloodiest war in American history were unleashed on Sumter. Major Anderson and his small command held out as long as they could, but after 34 hours of constant shelling they were forced to surrender. Anderson and his soldiers evacuated the fort at noon on the 14th. After firing a salute, they lowered the fort's main flag and marched out with dignity, "colors flying and drums beating," as their commander later recalled.

Following the surrender, Major Anderson was hailed as a hero at rallies throughout the North. Promoted to brigadier general on May 15, he was assigned to his native state of Kentucky, which he helped swing over to the North. Within a few months, health problems forced him to go on leave, however, and he resigned from active duty on October 17, 1863.

After the Union army recaptured Charleston, Anderson returned to Sumter on April 14, 1865, to raise the American flag that he had lowered four years earlier. General Anderson died while traveling in Nice, France, on October 26, 1871, and was subsequently given a hero's burial at the U.S. Military Academy at West Point, New York.

George Henry Thomas   1816 – 1870

★ ★ ★ ★ ★ ★ ★ ★ ★ ★ ★ ★ ★ ★

Today George H. Thomas is perhaps the least well-known of the North's great generals. A fine field commander who saved the Union from a disaster at the Battle of Chickamauga, Thomas was a quiet, deliberate leader whose lack of flamboyance kept him from achieving the widespread fame he truly deserved.

George Thomas was born on July 31, 1816, near Courtland, Virginia. After attending the local academy, Thomas studied law and served as a deputy court clerk until he was admitted to West Point in 1830. He graduated four years later, twelfth in a class that also included William T. Sherman and Richard S. Ewell. He was appointed to the

3rd U.S. Artillery and dispatched to Florida to fight the Seminoles. In 1846, during the Mexican War, Lieutenant Thomas was assigned to Gen. Zachary Taylor's command, earning commendations at Monterey and Buena Vista.

After the Mexican War, Thomas was promoted to captain and detailed as an artillery and cavalry instructor at West Point, where his deliberate, methodical style earned him the nickname "Old Slow Trot." In 1855, he was appointed major of the newly organized 2nd U.S. Cavalry, serving with the unit in Texas under Colonels Albert S. Johnston and Robert E. Lee.

When the crisis over Fort Sumter came to

a head in April 1861, George was on leave in the East. Unlike most of his fellow Virginians, he decided to remain loyal to the United States, a decision that cost him his home in Virginia and permanently divided his family (his sisters turned his picture to the wall and never spoke to him again, even

(opposite) George Thomas, displaying the fierce determination which earned him the title of the "Rock of Chickamauga."

(below) Thomas's troops in action at the Battle of Chickamauga. **They repulsed numerous Confederate assaults against their position on Snodgrass Hill on the afternoon of September 30, 1863, saving the Union Army from total defeat.**

The Confederate rout at the Battle of Mill Springs, Kentucky. Thomas's decisive victory there on January 19, 1862, removed all doubts about this Southern-born officer's loyalties.

General Thomas's headquarters in the beleaguered city of Chattanooga. Following the battle of Chickamauga, Thomas held this Tennessee stronghold against heavy Confederate opposition until Union reinforcements could arrive.

after the war). Reporting for duty in Pennsylvania on April 14, Thomas soon found himself colonel of the 2nd Cavalry following Johnston and Lee's resignations. In June he was assigned command of a brigade of infantry in the Shenandoah Valley. He remained in this Virginia hotbed through the First Battle of Bull Run. Then, on August 17, he was promoted to brigadier general, transferred to Kentucky, and placed in charge of a division.

As a native Southerner, General Thomas's loyalties were considered suspect early in the war; but after he defeated the Confederates at the Battle of Mill Springs, Kentucky, on January 19, 1862, all but the most cynical Northern leaders became convinced of his dedication to the Union cause. Appointed a major general on April 25, "Pap"—as his soldiers called him—next led his troops at the siege of Corinth, Mississippi, in May and June. Later reassigned to operations in Kentucky, he distinguished himself at the Battle of Perryville in October and Stones River in December. Thanks to these victories, he was awarded command of the 14th Corps, part of Gen. William Rosecrans's forces, on January 9, 1863.

During the ensuing months, Thomas, along with the rest of Rosecrans's command, was engaged in the task of driving Gen. Braxton Bragg's Confederates from Tennessee. It was during Bragg's decisive counterattack at the Battle of Chickamauga on September 19 and 20 that George Thomas rose to national prominence. When Bragg's army, aided by Gen. James Longstreet's corps, broke through Rosecrans's line on the second day of the battle, only Thomas held his position against the attacking rebels. His resolute stand saved the Union Army from a rout and earned him a new nickname, the "Rock of Chickamauga."

Following his defeat at Chickamauga, General Rosecrans retreated to Chattanooga, where his forces were soon besieged by Bragg's army. As a result "Old Rosey" was relieved of command of the Federal Army of the Cumberland on October 20 and replaced by Thomas, who assured Gen. Ulysses S. Grant that he would hold Chattanooga until reinforcements arrived—and did so, despite a rebel blockade that nearly starved his command. In the Battle of Missionary Ridge on

Thomas and Grant (standing, left) on Orchard Knob, outside Chattanooga. **From this high ground Thomas's troops captured the seemingly impregnable Confederate position on Missionary Ridge (background).**

November 25, Pap's understandably irate troops took the lead in driving Bragg's Southerners out of the city, winning a decisive victory for the Union.

After Chattanooga, General Thomas led the Army of the Cumberland south in Gen. William T. Sherman's Atlanta campaign, then headed into Tennessee in October to face Gen. John Hood's troops while Sherman began his March to the Sea. Although the Federal high command grew concerned that "Old Slow Trot" was taking much too long to move against Hood and almost replaced him, Thomas more than redeemed himself by annihilating Hood's army at the Battle of Nashville on December 15 and 16. In recog-

nition of his outstanding victory, Thomas was voted the thanks of Congress and earned a new sobriquet: the "sledge of Nashville."

General Thomas remained in command in Tennessee until the end of the war. At his request he was subsequently assigned command of the Military Department of the Pacific. George H. Thomas died on duty in San Francisco, California, on March 28, 1870.

Union monuments on Orchard Knob today.

BRIGADIER GENERAL

George Armstrong Custer   *1839 – 1876*

★   ★   ★   ★   ★   ★   ★   ★   ★   ★   ★   ★   ★

General Custer, one of the most colorful figures in American military history, in his trademark embroidered shirt, oversized cravat, and flowing curls. **His preference for this hair style led the Indians in the West to dub him "Long Hair."**

There are few figures in American military history as well known as George Armstrong Custer. Before he became the headstrong Indian fighter most people think of, however, he was one of the finest cavalry commanders in the Union Army and the youngest of the North's "boy generals."

Custer was born in New Rumley, Ohio, on December 5, 1839. After attending local schools, he was appointed to West Point in 1857 but was an uninspired student. Graduating last in his class in 1861 and avoiding dismissal for misconduct only because of the outbreak of the Civil War, he was commissioned a lieutenant in the 2nd U.S. Cavalry on June 24, 1861. Detailed to the defenses of the capital, Custer saw no combat in the first months of the war and finished the year on sick leave with his sister's family in Michigan.

Returning to Washington in time to join in Gen. George B. McClellan's Peninsular campaign the following March, Lieutenant Custer was assigned as a staff officer to Gen. William "Baldy" Smith. While on the Peninsula, Custer came to McClellan's attention when be became tired of listening to his superiors debate how deep the Chickahominy River was and rode his horse into the water to settle the question. McClellan, impressed by the young lieutenant's straightforward approach, had him appointed his aide on June 5.

After McClellan's dismissal, Custer was named to the staff of the Army of the Potomac's cavalry commander, Gen. Alfred Pleasonton. During the cavalry actions that followed—particularly the Battle of Aldie, Virginia, on June 17, 1863—Custer so impressed his commander with his leadership on the battlefield that Pleasonton had him promoted from lieutenant directly to brigadier general! Custer received his commission on June 29, 1863, when he was only 23 years old, thereby becoming the youngest Union general of the war.

Custer's Wolverines capturing some of Jeb Stuart's artillery near Culpeper, Virginia, in September 1863. By mid-war the initially ineffectual Union cavalrymen had become more than a match for Stuart's Confederates, largely as a result of the training they received from Custer and his fellow officers.

George Custer (left) with cavalry Gen. Alfred Pleasanton a few months before Custer's promotion to general.

"Custer's Last Stand" at the Battle of Little Bighorn, as depicted in Edgar S. Paxton's famous painting. Custer's rash assault against a Sioux encampment which vastly outnumbered his command has overshadowed his otherwise excellent record as a cavalry officer.

Custer was assigned command of a brigade of Michigan cavalry which he nicknamed his Wolverines. Leading them into combat less than a week later at the Battle of Gettysburg, he charged into Gen. Jeb Stuart's troopers east of town on July 3, driving them back in fierce combat. Custer's strong defense kept Stuart's rebel horsemen from disrupting the Union line on Cemetery Ridge during Pickett's Charge and confirmed George Custer as a splendid cavalry commander.

General Custer rose to his greatest wartime prominence after Philip H. Sheridan was appointed commander of the Army of the Potomac's Cavalry Corps in April 1864. On May 11, for example, in Sheridan's fight against Jeb Stuart's horsemen at Yellow Tavern, Virginia, it was Custer who led the charge that broke through the rebel lines and it was one of his Wolverines who killed General Stuart, inflicting an irreparable loss on the Southern war effort. During the subsequent Shenandoah Valley campaign, Custer played a pivotal role at the Battles of

Winchester and Cedar Creek, where he held the Union right throughout Gen. Jubal Early's surprise attack, giving Sheridan time to rally the rest of his scattered command and decisively defeat the Confederates. After spending the winter in the valley, General Custer—by that time commanding an entire division of troopers—succeeded in destroying the last remnants of Early's army at Waynesborough, Virginia, on March 2, capturing more than 1,600 soldiers.

With his victory in the Shenandoah Valley complete, Custer hurried to join the rest of Sheridan's command on the siege lines of Petersburg, Virginia. There he took a major role in the Battle of Five Forks on April 1 and led the ensuing Federal pursuit of Robert E. Lee's retreating rebels. On April 6 Custer's troopers captured one-third of what was left of the Army of Northern Virginia at Sayler's Creek, and two days later blocked Lee's final route of escape at Appomattox Court House. Finally, on the morning of April 9, it was George Custer who received a Southern courier bearing the news that General Lee wished to surrender to General Grant and end the war in Virginia. Custer

was later one of the officers present at the McLean house when the Confederate capitulation was worked out.

After the war Custer, the consummate cavalryman, went on to become one of the most famous Indian fighters in American history. While seeking to advance his military career—and, perhaps, his aspirations to the presidency—Custer led the 7th U.S. Cavalry in an attack on the Sioux Indian camp on the Little Big Horn River in Montana, on June 25, 1876. Although outnumbered, "Long Hair" refused to wait for reinforcements before engaging the Sioux, as he had been ordered to do, and was overrun and killed with all of his command in the most famous battle of the Indian Wars.

INTELLIGENCE AGENT
Elizabeth Van Lew   1822 – 1900

★ ★ ★ ★ ★ ★ ★ ★ ★ ★ ★ ★ ★ ★

While the Confederacy had numerous sympathizers in the North to serve as spies, women like Belle Boyd and Rose Greenhow, the Union did not have many supporters in the South to help its cause. For much of the war, the U.S. government had only one agent in Richmond, an unmarried lady in her forties, Miss Elizabeth Van Lew, but she was enough. Thanks to her resourcefulness, the Yankees stayed well informed about the activities in the Confederate capital throughout the war, earning Lizzie the personal thanks of Ulysses S. Grant.

Elizabeth Van Lew was born into a wealthy family of Richmond, Virginia, around 1822, but she received her schooling in Philadelphia, Pennsylvania, where she became a dedicated abolitionist. After her father's death in 1847, she not only convinced her mother to free their slaves but went on to buy some of the freedmen's family members from other owners in order to liberate them as well. These manumissions were frowned upon by the Van Lews's upper-class friends, but they earned Lizzie the trust of blacks throughout the area, creating valuable allies who helped in her dangerous work during the war.

Even before the onset of hostilities in 1861, Miss Van Lew began sending reports of secessionist activities in Virginia to Washington, D.C., developing contacts she would use throughout the four years of fighting. She proved a clever, skillful agent, concealing ciphered messages in hollow eggs, in quilting, and her servants' clothing. She often divided the coded letters into pieces so they could be more easily hidden, and was never caught.

After the Union defeat at First Bull Run in July 1861, Miss Van Lew used her family connections to get permission to tend the captured Federal officers in Richmond's Libby Prison. She brought them food and medicine and often smuggled out messages for their families, sometimes spelled out by

Elizabeth Van Lew, the Union's unlikely master spy in Richmond.

pinpricks laboriously placed under letters in books she lent the prisoners. Her attention to these Yankees led some to accuse her of being a Northern agent and to call for her arrest. Rather than deny the accusations, however, she continued to openly help the Federal soldiers, making her behavior so obvious that it seemed impossible for her to be a spy. Later, she began to purposely dress in a disheveled manner and talk to herself in public, thus earning the nickname "Crazy Bet." This behavior further threw off suspicion about her activities.

Meanwhile, Miss Van Lew gathered her information from contacts throughout Richmond. She had agents in the Confederate War Department and the Congress and even managed to get a former slave hired as a maid in the Confederate White House to spy on Jefferson Davis. Her intelligence proved invaluable to the Union cause and was always reliable.

In addition to securing information for the Yankees, "Crazy Bet" harbored fugitives in secret rooms in her home and in other safe houses in the area. Her greatest triumph

occurred in February 1864 when she helped hide some of the 109 Union prisoners who had tunneled out of Libby Prison.

After the Union army commenced operations outside of Petersburg, Virginia, in June 1864, Miss Van Lew's couriers not only kept Gen. U.S. Grant thoroughly informed of activities in Richmond, they brought flowers from her garden for his headquarters as well. When the Confederate capital finally fell to the Yankees on April 2, 1865, Grant dispatched troops to protect the Van Lew house and later called on its mistress to personally thank her for her help.

After the war, Miss Van Lew was appointed Postmistress of Richmond for eight years as a reward for her loyalty to the Union. Subsequently impoverished, she was supported by the families of some of the officers she had aided in Libby Prison. Elizabeth Van Lew died in Richmond in 1900 and is memorialized by a monument declaring "She risked everything that was dear to her . . . that slavery might be abolished and the Union preserved."

George Gordon Meade 1815 – 1872

★ ★ ★ ★ ★ ★ ★ ★ ★ ★ ★ ★ ★ ★ ★

George G. Meade is probably the most underrated of the Union's leading generals. A first-class division and corps commander and the man who directed the Army of the Potomac's first decisive victory at Gettysburg, Meade's contribution to the North's war effort has been largely overshadowed by late-war giants such as Ulysses S. Grant, William T. Sherman, and Philip H. Sheridan.

George Meade was born on December 31, 1815, in Cádiz, Spain, where his father Richard, a merchant, was serving as naval agent for the U.S. government. Brought to the United States by his mother six months later, George spent his youth in Pennsylvania and Washington, D.C., where his father fought unsuccessfully to recover a substantial amount owed him by the government. When Richard died in 1828, his family was left in

poor financial condition and George turned to the U.S. Military Academy as an inexpensive way of gaining a college education. Admitted to West Point in 1831, Meade graduated 19th out of 56 cadets in 1835 and was assigned to the artillery. After serving the minimum one-year tour of duty, he resigned his commission in October 1836 to become a surveyor and engineer.

Following his wedding to Margaretta Sergeant in 1840, Meade applied to rejoin the Army. On May 19, 1842, he was commissioned a lieutenant in the elite Topographical Engineers. Except for a brief tour of duty in the Mexican War, he spent most of the next 20 years as a surveyor for the government, rising to the rank of captain in 1856.

After the First Battle of Bull Run, Meade was appointed a brigadier general of volunteers on August 31, 1861, and placed in command of a brigade of Pennsylvanians, serving in the same division as John Reynolds. The following March, after several

months of training near Washington, D.C., General Meade's troops were dispatched to the Virginia Peninsula to take part in George McClellan's Richmond campaign. During the Seven Days' Battles in June, Meade proved that he could do more for the Army than just survey. Indeed, he led his troops with valor at Mechanicsville, Gaines' Mill, and White Oak Swamp, where he remained on the field despite two severe wounds.

Although not yet recovered from his injuries, Meade insisted on rejoining his brigade for the Second Battle of Bull Run in August. During the Antietam campaign in September, he temporarily succeeded Gen. John Reynolds as commander of their division, earning a commendation for his actions at the Battle of South Mountain on the 14th. At Antietam three days later, his troops undertook a two-hour assault at the battlefield's Bloody Lane, retiring only when they ran out of ammunition. After Gen. Joseph Hooker was wounded later in the day, Meade took charge of the entire First Corps and, in recognition of his exemplary service, was promoted to major general on November 29. Meade's finest hour as a field commander occurred at the Battle of Fredericksburg on December 13, when he directed the only Federal assault to break the Confederate line south of the city. Following this engagement, he was awarded command of the 5th Corps, which he led with distinction through the Battle of Chancellorsville in May 1863.

After General Hooker's defeat at Chancellorsville, Abraham Lincoln sought a new commander for the Army of the Potomac. When the President's first choice, John Reynolds, refused the position, Lincoln

General Meade and his staff after the Battle of Gettysburg. **Running the army required an extensive staff system including couriers, personal aides, and specialists such as signal officers, doctors, engineers, and paymasters.**

(opposite) Maj. Gen. George Meade, commander of the Army of the Potomac for the last two years of the war. **His beak-like nose and hair-trigger temper led his officers to call him "the old snapping turtle."**

Fredericksburg, Virginia, from the South. While a division commander, Meade led the only Federal troops to break through the Confederate line here during the Battle of Fredericksburg.

Meade's headquarters at Gettysburg. The tiny cottage was severely damaged in the artillery barrage that preceeded Pickett's charge on the third day of the battle.

The Battle of the Wilderness. **General-in-Chief Ulysses S. Grant attached himself to the Army of the Potomac in March 1864, effectively superseding Meade as commander of the Army from this battle until the end of the war.**

turned to Meade, appointing him to the post on June 8. George Meade assumed command while the Federal forces were pursuing Robert E. Lee's troops into Pennsylvania, and after just three days the Union general found himself in the unenviable position of leading his soldiers into combat against a foe who had never been beaten. In the Battle of Gettysburg which ensued on July 1–3 Meade directed his forces with tact and skill, placing great faith in corps commanders like Winfield Hancock and Oliver Howard but making all the final decisions himself. Under his leadership, the Union Army won its first victory over Lee's Army of Northern Virginia, making

George Meade a national hero and earning him a vote of thanks by Congress.

Meade remained commanding general of the Army of the Potomac for the rest of the war, but after Ulysses S. Grant was appointed general-in-chief of the Union forces on March 12, 1864, Meade was effectively superseded as that Army's leader. Unlike many Union generals, Meade was professional enough to not let such matters bother him overmuch, and he continued to serve the Union with distinction until the end of the war.

After Lee's surrender at Appomattox Court House in April 1865, Meade remained in the Army, serving in administrative posts in Georgia and Pennsylvania. He died while on duty in Philadelphia on November 6, 1872.

Gouverneur Kemble Warren   1830 – 1882

★ ★ ★ ★ ★ ★ ★ ★ ★ ★ ★ ★ ★

The story of Gouverneur Warren is the most tragic of any leading Union general. A fine soldier who played a pivotal role in the Battle of Gettysburg, Warren was unjustly relieved of command a few days before the end of the war. He spent the rest of his life trying to clear his record but died a bitter man without vindication.

Warren was born on January 8, 1830, in Cold Spring, New York, which lies across the Hudson River from West Point. The scion of a prominent family, he was named after a local congressman and business magnate, Gouverneur Kemble. Warren was admitted to the U.S. Military Academy at age 16 and graduated second in his class in 1850. Appointed to the exclusive Corps of Topographical Engineers, he was assigned to surveying details in the West until August 1859, when he was named assistant professor of mathematics at West Point.

With the coming of the Civil War, Warren left his post at the Military Academy to become lieutenant colonel of New York's Duryée Zouaves on May 14, 1861. This colorful unit, resplendent in red and blue uniforms complete with turbans, became one of the most famous regiments in the Union Army after it spearheaded the first battle of the war at Big Bethel, Virginia, on June 10. Warren, who was promoted to colonel that September, rose to prominence along with his unit, and in May 1862 was assigned command of his entire brigade.

Colonel Warren led his new command through most of the Peninsular campaign that spring, winning a commendation for bravery at the Battle of Gaines' Mill on June 27. At the Second Battle of Bull Run on August 30, he directed his unit in one of the most valiant stands of the war when they held off the attack of Gen. James Longstreet's numerically superior Confederates long enough for the Yankees to establish a fallback position on Henry House Hill. It was a terribly costly engagement, however, resulting in the death of one quarter of the Duryée Zouaves—the highest unit loss by percentage in any battle of the war. In recognition of this heroic defense, Warren was named a brigadier general on September 26.

In March 1863 General Warren was appointed chief engineer of the Army of the Potomac and was subsequently promoted to major general. While serving in this position on Gen. George G. Meade's staff at Gettysburg, he performed his most important act of the Civil War. Riding out to inspect the far left of the Union line during the Confederate advance on the afternoon of July 2, he was appalled to find the high ground there—a hill called Little Round Top—unoccupied except for a few Federal signalmen. The experienced engineer immediately realized that if the rebels placed artillery on the rise they could shell the entire Union line, driving the Yankees from Gettysburg in defeat. On his own initiative, he ordered the first troops that he encountered—among them Col.

(opposite) **Gouverneur Warren, the savior of Little Round Top at Gettysburg.** This highly capable Union officer was unfairly removed from corps command just days before the end of the war.

(left) *General Warren and his 5th Corps staff at their field headquarters in 1864.*

Josiah Chamberlain's 20th Maine Infantry— to hold Little Round Top at all costs. His decisiveness, coming only moments before the arrival of Longstreet's lead units, prevented a strategic disaster that could have ended the war for the North.

After the Battle of Gettysburg, General Warren was assigned temporary command of the Army's 2nd Corps in place of the wounded Gen. Winfield Hancock. He served with distinction in this capacity until March 24, 1864, when he was awarded permanent command of the 5th Corps, which he led through Grant's Virginia campaign in May and the siege of Petersburg in June. Toward the end of that ten-month standoff, on April 1, 1865, Warren was ordered to move his corps to the southern end of the Union line to support Gen. Philip H. Sheridan's cavalry in an attack on the vital Confederate position at Five Forks. Due to faulty instructions, Warren arrived late and marched by the wrong road, attacking the Confederates at the rear rather than the front. Although this maneuver clearly helped win the battle, Sheridan was incensed at Warren's errors and immediately removed him from command. Transferred to Mississippi, General Warren ended the war without glory as commander in Vicksburg.

Warren remained in the Army as an engineer after the war, doing surveys and pressing for an open investigation of his performance at Five Forks. A court of inquiry eventually exonerated him of all charges, but it was a hollow victory; it came three months after the general's death in Newport, Rhode Island, on August 8, 1882. Bitter over his treatment after a lifetime of service to the Army, Warren refused to be buried in his uniform and specified that no military rituals be performed at his funeral.

The summit of Little Round Top, displaying its commanding position over the surrounding countryside. **General Warren's pivotal role in saving this position during the battle in July 1863 is commemorated by a statue which overlooks Plum Run Valley toward Devil's Den.**

REAR ADMIRAL
David Dixon Porter   *1813 – 1891*

★ ★ ★ ★ ★ ★ ★ ★ ★ ★ ★ ★ ★

No family in American history has done more for the U.S. Navy than David Porter's. The son and grandson of Naval officers, brother of Capt. William "Dirty Bill" Porter and foster brother of Adm. David Glasgow Farragut, David Porter made his mark at Vicksburg and Fort Fisher and finished the war second only to Farragut as the nation's leading Naval hero.

The future admiral was born in Chester, Pennsylvania, on June 8, 1813 to Commo. David Porter, a hero of the War of 1812, and Evelina Anderson Porter. During the Mexican War for Independence against Spain in the 1820s, Commodore Porter joined the Mexican Navy and arranged for his son David to be appointed a midshipman in his fleet at age 13. Captured in combat off the Cuban coast, young David returned to the United States in 1829 and was named a midshipman in the U.S. Navy. He spent the next 18 years on duty in the Mediterranean and surveying the American coast.

During the Mexican-American War, the junior Porter—by then a lieutenant—commanded a landing party at Tabasco, winning a commendation from Commo. Matthew Perry for capturing the Mexican fort there. After the war, Porter took an extended leave to enter the merchant marine. He returned to the Navy in 1855, but was dissatisfied with his administrative assignments and by 1861 had made up his mind to leave the service. As the secession crisis heightened, however, Porter was reassigned to shipboard command. On April 1, 1861, he was ordered to support Fort Pickens, Florida, a Union stronghold that was in a beleaguered state similar to that of Fort Sumter in South Carolina. Lieutenant Porter's mission was canceled just as he reached the Florida coast, but he had proven himself an energetic, dedicated Union man and was promoted two grades to full commander

Adm. David Porter, the Naval hero of Vicksburg.

Porter's fleet anchored off of Vicks-burg after the city's surrender on July 4, 1863. **Shelling from these ships had added immeasurably to the effectiveness of the Union siege here.**

effective April 22. He spent the rest of the year supervising blockades of Gulf ports and pursuing the Confederate raider *Sumter* off the coast of South America.

The following spring, Commander Porter had a major role in planning the assault on New Orleans and was instrumental in his foster brother David Farragut's appointment as head of the expedition. While the rest of Farragut's fleet moved north to take New Orleans, Porter's mortar boats pounded the city's outlying defenses until they capitulated on April 27. Following the surrender of New Orleans, Porter joined Farragut on his reconnaissance cruise up the Mississippi to explore the defenses of Vicksburg.

David Porter's fighting record and experience at Vicksburg made him a natural choice as commander of the Federal fleet on the upper Mississippi River following Flag Officer Andrew Foote's departure. Appointed on October 9 with the rank of acting rear admiral, Porter was soon in the thick of Gen. Ulysses S. Grant's Vicksburg campaign. His gunboats first played a pivotal role in the capture of Confederate Fort Hindman at

Arkansas Post, Arkansas, on January 10–11, 1863, thereby opening the Mississippi River to Federal traffic as far south as the Arkansas River. Thereafter, Grant's troops marched down the west bank of the Mississippi River opposite Vicksburg, while Porter led part of his fleet past the high bluffs on which were arrayed the city's extensive defenses on the evening of April 16. After a two-hour battle, Porter got his entire fleet, except for one transport, safely south of Vicksburg. Continuing on to Bruinsburg, Mississippi, his vessels ferried Grant's soldiers across to the east bank of the river, opening the way for their fight through Mississippi. During the ensuing siege of Vicksburg, Porter's gunboats and mortars constantly shelled the city from the river, contributing significantly to the city's fall on July 4. In recognition of his outstanding cooperation and daring leadership during this campaign, Porter was promoted to the permanent rank of rear admiral and voted the thanks of Congress.

Porter continued to serve on the Mississippi River for a year. Then, in October 1864, he was given charge of the blockade of the Atlantic coast. By that time, the Confederates had only one functioning port, at Wil-

mington, North Carolina. Ordered to capture the heavily defended city, David organized a joint Army–Navy assault that involved more than 60 ships—the largest fleet of war vessels ever assembled by the United States to that time. This armada succeeded in capturing Fort Fisher, which guarded the entrance to the harbor, on January 15, 1865, and Wilmington fell with the arrival of Gen. John Schofield's troops on February 22, closing the South's last entryway for supplies.

Admiral Porter finished the war commanding the fleet on the James River outside Richmond, touring the fallen city with President Lincoln on April 4. After the Confederate surrender Porter was appointed superintendent of the U.S. Naval Academy, earning a promotion to vice admiral on July 25, 1866. In the years that followed, he served as adviser to the Navy Department, making many improvements in that branch of service, and rose to the rank of full admiral on August 15, 1870. After a naval career of more than 60 years, David Porter died at his home in Washington, D.C., on February 13, 1891.

Francis Channing Barlow   1834 – 1896

★ ★ ★ ★ ★ ★ ★ ★ ★ ★ ★ ★ ★ ★

The pressing need for officers during the Civil War enabled many young men in their twenties and thirties to attain generalship. Probably the best of the Union's "boy generals" was Francis Barlow, an intelligent young lawyer from New York who served with distinction from the beginning of the war through Appomattox.

Barlow was born in Brooklyn, New York, on October 19, 1834, the son of Unitarian clergyman David Barlow. When Francis was two, his family moved to Brookline, Massachusetts, where he was raised. He entered Harvard in 1851, graduated fours years later, and went to New York to study law. The brilliant young attorney passed the bar in 1858 and quickly developed a lucrative practice.

After war was declared on April 15, 1861, Barlow immediately enlisted in the 12th New York Infantry, turning down the offer of a commission to start as a private. Francis departed for Washington, D.C., on April 20, just one day after his wedding to Arabella Wharton Griffith. He served in the capital and in the Shenandoah Valley for three months and was promoted to first lieutenant before he was mustered out of the 90-day unit on August 1.

Barlow reenlisted as a lieutenant colonel of the 61st New York Infantry on November 9. Appointed its colonel the following April, he led the unit throughout the Peninsular campaign, gaining distinction at the Battle of Fair Oaks on May 31. Francis subsequently earned his promotion to brigadier general at the Battle of Antietam in September, where he was severely wounded while leading his men at the battlefield's "Bloody Lane."

After recovering his health under the care of his wife, who was serving as a volunteer Army nurse, General Barlow was assigned a brigade in Gen. Oliver Howard's 11th Corps.

Francis Barlow, one of several "boy generals" in the Union Army. His clean-shaven, youthful face made him appear even younger than his 27 years.

Assuming command on April 17, 1863, his brigade received its baptism of fire a few weeks later at the Battle of Chancellorsville, when it was routed with the rest of the 11th Corps by Stonewall Jackson's surprise attack on May 2.

Barlow and his soldiers redeemed themselves at the Battle of Gettysburg. On July 1, they held their position—north of town at the far right of the Union line—for more than two hours under heavy Confederate fire. Finally, Gen. Jubal Early's rebels outflanked their right—a hill now known as Barlow's Knoll—and they were forced to retreat, but not until they had done some of the best fighting in the 11th Corps that day.

During the struggle around the knoll, General Barlow was again seriously wounded. Left on the battlefield, he was discovered by some passing Southern officers who gave him water and had him moved to safety (in later years the Confederate commander in that sector, Gen. James Gordon, claimed that he had helped Francis, but there is no evidence to sustain his story). The following day Barlow's wife arrived at Gettysburg. She worked her way through the Con-

federate lines until she found her husband, and again nursed him to recovery after Lee's forces abandoned Gettysburg.

Francis was finally well enough to return to duty on March 25, 1864, when he was assigned command of a division in Winfield Hancock's 2nd Corps. His finest service of the war came shortly thereafter during the Battle of Spotsylvania, when he led the Union assault at the battlefield's "Mule Shoe" salient on May 12. After a full day of intense hand-to-hand combat, his men broke through the rebel line, capturing more than 3,000 prisoners, 20 cannon, and 30 battle flags.

Following his success at Spotsylvania, General Barlow accompanied the 2nd Corps on the Army of the Potomac's march to Petersburg, Virginia. The siege there proved too much for his health, however, and after his wife's unexpected death on July 27, he went on an extended leave. He rejoined the Army on April 6, 1865, taking part in the pursuit of Lee's forces to Appomattox Court House. Following the surrender, Barlow was placed in command of the 2nd Corps and subsequently promoted to major general on May 25.

General Barlow resigned from the Army on November 16 to return to his law practice. In later years he served as New York secretary of state and attorney general, earning accolades for his prosecution of the corrupt New York City politician "Boss" Tweed. Francis Barlow died in New York City on January 11, 1896, and is buried in Brookline, Massachusetts.

Abraham Lincoln   1809 – 1865

★ ★ ★ ★ ★ ★ ★ ★ ★ ★ ★ ★ ★

Abraham Lincoln was the central figure of the Civil War: his election was the direct cause of the conflict; his unwavering dedication to the Union steered its course; and he died a martyr at its conclusion, becoming an American hero second only to George Washington.

Abraham Lincoln was born on February 12, 1809, near Hodgenville, Kentucky, the son of Thomas Lincoln, a poor farmer, and Nancy Hanks Lincoln. Abe spent his childhood in the backwoods of Kentucky and Indiana, helping his father with the farmwork and getting a very limited schooling. As a young man he worked as a farm laborer and flatboatman, traveling down the Mississippi River to New Orleans, where he first encountered slavery up close. In 1832, he moved to New Salem, Illinois, and became a storekeeper. He took advantage of his time there to better his education, reading voraciously and joining the local debating society. He quickly developed an interest in politics and the law, and in 1834 won his first of four terms as a state legislator on the Whig ticket. Three years later he was admitted to the bar and moved to Springfield, where he became known as a brilliant attorney. He married Mary Todd on November 4, 1842, and was elected to the U.S. House of Representatives as a Whig in 1846. Defeated for reelection two years later, he returned to Springfield and resumed his law practice.

Abe became a supporter of the newly established Republican Party in 1856. In 1858 he ran as the Republican candidate for the U.S. Senate from Illinois, and although he lost the election to the Democratic incumbent, Stephen A. Douglas, his superb performance in his widely publicized series of debates with his opponent catapulted him to national attention. Two years later "Honest Abe" received the Republican nomination for President; he went on to defeat Stephen Douglas, John Bell, and John C. Breckinridge in a four-way race in November. (He failed to capture a majority of the popular vote but garnered 180 votes in the electoral college,

Abraham Lincoln as he appeared in the 1850s. He did not grow his beard until the 1860 Presidential campaign, when 11-year-old Grace Bedell of Westfield, New York, wrote him to suggest that he consider growing whiskers.

more than enough to ensure his election.)

Lincoln's election as the first Republican President sent a shockwave through the slave states of the South. Although he ran on a platform that called for banning slavery only in the Western territories and not in the states where it already existed, most Southerners saw any move to limit their "peculiar institution" as an unconstitutional step toward abolition. In response, seven Southern states seceded from the Union before Lincoln was even sworn in as 16th President of the United States on March 4, 1861.

Lincoln knew that his first task as President was to demonstrate his deep commitment to preserving the Union, but at the same time he did not wish to take an aggressive stand against the South. Accordingly, he announced that he would send a relief expedition to the Union garrison at Fort Sumter, South Carolina, which was besieged by forces under Gen. P. G. T. Beauregard, but would not have it fire upon the local insurrectionists unless fired upon first. He thereby put the responsibility for starting or avoiding war on the South. The Confederacy responded by

(opposite) **Lincoln with his beloved youngest son Thomas, whom the President called "Tad," short for "Tadpole."**

(above) President Lincoln photographed with Gen. John McClernand (right) and Allan Pinkerton, founder of the Pinkerton Detective Agency and the Army's chief of intelligence. This photo was taken during Lincoln's visit to the headquarters of the Army of the Potomac in November 1862. Lincoln seldom took to the field, preferring not to meddle in his generals' operations.

(right) Lincoln's home in Springfield, Illinois, preserved today as a museum. It was the only house the President and Mary Todd Lincoln ever owned.

capturing Sumter before the Union ships could arrive, and on April 15 President Lincoln declared that a state of war existed between the North and the South and called for 75,000 troops to put down the Southern rebellion.

Lincoln proved himself to be a remarkable wartime leader, displaying the ability to be alternately diplomatic and forceful with an innate sense of when to compromise and when to be steadfast in his convictions. Although he had no formal military training, Lincoln also proved himself to be an insightful commander-in-chief, recognizing what many of his generals failed to grasp— that their prime mission was to cripple the South's ability to wage war, not just to capture its capital city. Unlike Confederate President Jefferson Davis, however, Lincoln almost never interfered with his generals in the field; he would advise them or urge them to action, but in the end the decisions were theirs, and if they failed to favorably advance

the conduct of the war, he tried someone else. With patience and fortitude he endured two grueling years of failures and defeats before finally finding the generals who would win the war for him.

At the outset of the conflict, Lincoln, who was not a doctrinal abolitionist, saw the Civil War primarily as a struggle to reunite the Union and was willing to let the South keep its slaves. When it became apparent, however, that slavery was the central issue undergirding the Confederacy's will to fight, he resolved to position the North on the side of freedom. On September 22, 1862, he issued the Emancipation Proclamation, which freed the slaves in the Confederate States. Thereafter, the Great Emancipator was firmly committed to equal rights for all African-Americans.

After four years of war, Lincoln seriously feared defeat in his bid for reelection in 1864, but following Gen. William T. Sherman's victory at Atlanta in September, he easily won against his Democratic challenger,

The assassination of Abraham Lincoln at Ford's Theatre on April 14, 1865. **This dire act by John Wilkes Booth didn't rally the South as the actor expected. Instead it made the defeated Confederates fearful of Northern retaliation.**

former Gen. George B. McClellan. In little more than a month after his second inaugural on March 4, 1865, Lee surrendered to Grant at Appomattox Court House and Lincoln began turning his attention toward the task of national reunification. His plans for reconciliation "with malice toward none; with charity for all" were not to be, however. They ended with a shot from an assassin's pistol at Ford's Theater in Washington, D.C., on the evening of April 14. Mortally wounded by John Wilkes Booth, an actor and Southern sympathizer, President Lincoln died the next morning, and a shocked nation mourned. After a series of state funerals in cities from Washington to Chicago, Abraham Lincoln was finally laid to rest in Springfield, Illinois, on May 4, 1865.

MAJOR GENERAL
John Sedgwick   *1813 – 1864*

John Sedgwick may have been the most popular general in the Union Army, and he was certainly one of its best fighters. Known affectionately as "Uncle John" to his men, Sedgwick was a fearless soldier who served with distinction as a division and corps commander from the Peninsular campaign until his death at Spotsylvania.

John was born in the small village of Cornwall Hollow, Connecticut, on September 13, 1813. He received his basic education in local schools and the academy at Sharon, Connecticut, then entered West Point in 1833. Upon his graduation in the middle of his class in 1837, Sedgwick was commissioned a lieutenant of artillery and dispatched to Florida for service during the Seminole War. Following several years of garrison duty, he was given a field command during the Mexican War, earning commendations for bravery at the Battles of Churubusco and Chapultepec. After the war he was assigned to fight Indians in the Western territories, and in 1855 was promoted to major and transferred to the newly established 1st U.S. Cavalry.

At the beginning of the Civil War Sedgwick—by then a lieutenant colonel—was serving with the cavalry at Fort Wise, Colorado. Ordered east, he was promoted to brigadier general on August 31, 1861, and given command of a brigade in the Army of the Potomac on October 3. Four months later, on February 9, 1862, the veteran soldier was placed in charge of a division in the Army's 2nd Corps.

"Uncle John" first led his troops into combat during Gen. George B. McClellan's Peninsular campaign that spring, fighting with particular bravery at Yorktown, at Fair Oaks, and at White Oak Swamp, where he was badly wounded. In recognition of his fine performance in the field, Sedgwick was

John Sedgwick, the genial general whom his soldiers called "Uncle John."

The scene of General Sedgwick's death at Spotsylvania, May 9, 1864. **Shot in the head by a sniper, he died almost instantly.**

promoted to major general on July 4. Returning to duty for the battle of Antietam on September 17, he further distinguished himself by leading an attack into the West Wood on the morning of the fight. Surprised there by Gen. Lafayette McLaws's Confederates, Sedgwick sustained three wounds while trying to rally his badly mauled troops and finally had to be carried from the field, with Gen. Oliver Howard succeeding to his command.

After his recovery in December, General Sedgwick was successively awarded command of the 2nd, 9th, and 6th Corps, remaining with the latter from February 4, 1863, until his death. During the Battle of Chancellorsville, his troops captured the city of Fredericksburg on May 3, successfully storming the rebel position at Marye's Heights that had seemed impregnable in the Battle of Fredericksburg in December. On

the following day, they held off Lee's final assault during the battle at Salem Church, midway between Fredericksburg and Chancellorsville.

Sedgwick's most remarkable contribution to the Union cause occurred during the Battle of Gettysburg. When the general received word that fighting had broken out late on July 1, his corps was 34 miles away in Maryland. Inspiring his men to a superhuman effort, "Uncle John" marched them all night and throughout the following day until they arrived at Gettysburg around 5 P.M. Without pausing for rest, Sedgwick threw them into combat near Little Round Top, helping to secure that strategic position for the North.

After Gettysburg, "Uncle John" continued to win accolades for his leadership at the Battle of Rappahannock Station on November 7 and at the Wilderness on May 5 and 6, 1864. While posting his artillery at the subsequent battle of Spotsylvania on May 9, General Sedgwick was killed by a Confederate sniper just moments after assuring his aides that the rebels "couldn't hit an elephant at this distance." John Sedgwick has since been memorialized by statues at West Point and Gettysburg.

Daniel Edgar Sickles   1825 – 1914

★　★　★　★　★　★　★　★　★　★　★　★

Daniel Sickles is probably the most controversial figure in this book. A brash, self-important political appointee, Sickles advanced without orders at Gettysburg, destroying his command. But he very likely saved the Union Army from a disastrous Confederate flank attack in the process.

Sickles was born in New York City on October 20, 1825. After graduating from the University of the City of New York (now NYU), he began studying law and was admitted to the bar in 1846. Entering Democratic politics, he served as a New York State assemblyman and senator and as secretary to the U.S. legation in London under Ambassador James Buchanan.

In 1856, Sickles was elected to his first term in Congress. While in Washington he became embroiled in scandal by killing his wife's lover, Philip Barton Key—the son of *Star Spangled Banner* composer Francis Scott Key—on February 27, 1859. Sickles's lawyer, future Attorney General and Secretary of War Edwin Stanton, pled temporary insanity for his jealous client and Dan was acquitted. It was the first time that line of defense had ever been used in an American courtroom.

As the secession crisis came to a head in December 1860, Congressman Sickles and his friend Stanton—by then President Buchanan's attorney general—urged Buchanan not to abandon the beleaguered Fort Sumter, in Charleston, South Carolina. When Sumter finally fell and war was declared in April 1861 Sickles, a staunch Unionist, rushed to organize a command in New York. He received permission from Edwin Morgan, New York's Republican governor, to recruit a regiment but rapidly signed up troops for an entire brigade. Morgan, not wishing to appoint the former Democratic congressman a brigadier general, refused to acknowledge Sickles's volunteers, but President Lincoln, recognizing the need for Democratic support

for the war, accepted his Excelsior Brigade as Federal volunteers and had Sickles commissioned a brigadier general on September 3, 1861. Although he had no military background General Sickles proved to be a tough fighter, serving with distinction at the Battle of Fair Oaks and at Oak Grove during the Peninsular campaign the following spring.

At the conclusion of the Peninsular campaign in July 1862, General Sickles returned to New York to bolster the war effort there. On rejoining his command in October, he was placed in charge of a division in the Army of the Potomac's 3rd Corps and promoted to major general on November 29; two months later he was appointed corps commander. Sickles again showed himself to be an aggressive, insightful leader at the Battle of Chancellorsville, fought on May 1–4, 1863. Spotting Stonewall Jackson's troops on their flank march around the Union Army on May 2, Sickles requested permission to attack but was held back until late afternoon. When he finally received word to advance, it was too late to stop Jackson, but Sickles did secure a strategically important rise south of Chancellorsville called Hazel Dell. During

(opposite) The self-confident (and self-important) Brig. Gen. Daniel Sickles. **A political appointee, he nevertheless turned out to be a good fighting general.**

the Confederate assault the following day, Sickles was ordered to retreat and against his better judgment he abandoned Hazel Dell, allowing Confederate troops under Gen. James Archer to place artillery there and drive the Yankees from Chancellorsville. Afterward, Sickles never forgot what his obedience to orders had cost the Army that day.

That experience played a particularly significant role in sparking his controversial actions at the Battle of Gettysburg on July 2, 1863. Posted at the southern end of the Union line on Cemetery Ridge, Sickles felt that the position was too extended and low-lying for the 3rd Corps to protect. After his requests to advance to higher ground a half mile to the west were rejected, Sickles finally ordered the move on his own, vowing that he would not suffer another Chancellorsville. His troops reached the battlefield's Peach Orchard and Devil's Den just in time to

Troops of Sickles's Excelsior Brigade charging the Confederates during the Battle of Fair Oaks in 1862.

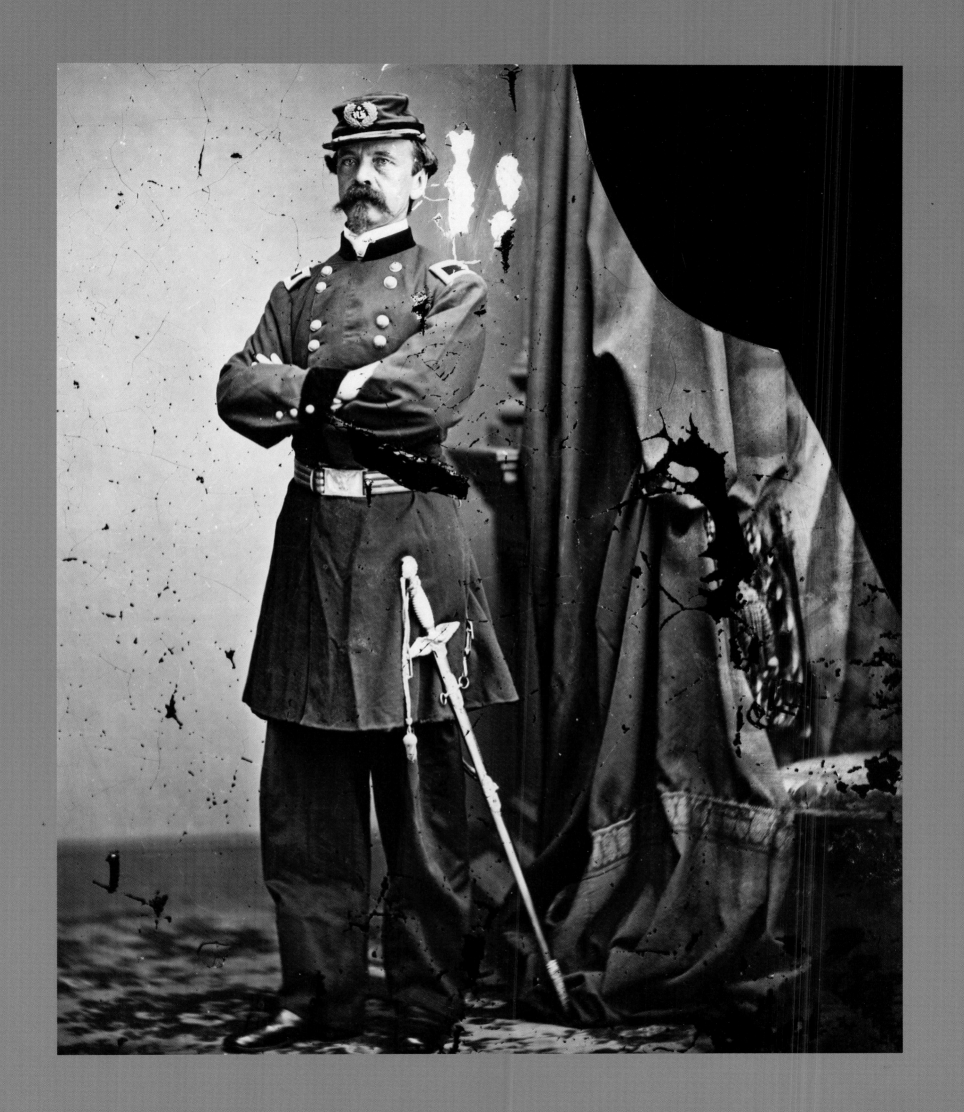

The Peach Orchard, as preserved today in the Gettysburg National Military Park. The round-topped monument (right rear) marks the Excelsior Brigade's position during the fighting here.

block Gen. James Longstreet's surprise attack against the Federal left flank. The loss to Sickles's corps was devastating as his men bore the brunt of the rebel assault, but they gave the Yankees time to secure their left flank at Little Round Top and probably saved the Union Army from disaster.

General Sickles was badly wounded in his right leg during the fight near the Peach Orchard. Carried from the field on a stretcher, he insisted on smoking a cigar so his men would know he wasn't dead. When the limb had to be amputated, he donated it to the Army Medical Museum in Washington, D.C. In later years he occasionally went there to view his shattered bones, which are still on display.

After his recovery Sickles was assigned to administrative duties and never allowed to return to field command. During the Recon-

struction period he served as military governor of the Carolinas (1865–1867) and later as Ambassador to Spain (1869–1873). Daniel Sickles died in New York City on May 3, 1914.

General Sickles in Washington, D.C., after the amputation of his leg. With him is Gen. Samuel Heintzelman, commander of the capital's defenses.

Mary Ann Ball Bickerdyke   *1817 – 1901*

Most of the women who rose to prominence as nurses during the Civil War were genteel, well-educated ladies like Clara Barton and Sally Tompkins. But one of the North's best volunteer nurses was a rough-hewn Illinois widow whom the soldiers lovingly called "Mother"—Mary Ann Bickerdyke.

Mary Ball was born near Mount Vernon, Ohio, on July 19, 1817, the daughter of Hiram and Anna Rodgers Ball. Her mother died the year after her birth, and Mary was raised by her grandfather, John Rodgers, a local farmer and Revolutionary War veteran.

Mary moved to Oberlin, Ohio, in 1833, and may have attended Oberlin College. Four years later, she went to Cincinnati, where she studied herbal medicine at Dr. Zimri Hussey's Physio-Botanic Medical College. After graduating, she married Robert Bickerdyke, a painter and musician, on April 27, 1847, and eventually settled in Galesburg, Illinois. When Robert died in 1858, Mary, always a self-reliant woman, supported her family as a practicing botanic physician.

Shortly after the beginning of the Civil War, Mary's church sponsored a meeting to discuss the poor camp conditions of the local volunteers. Mrs. Bickerdyke was asked to see to the men's needs and, on June 9, 1861, she traveled to the fort at Cairo, Illinois to embark on a mission that would last for the rest of the war. Appalled at the conditions in the camp hospital, the 44-year-old widow quickly took charge, cleaning both the facility and its inmates thoroughly over the protests of the base's inexperienced surgeons. In the process, she earned the nickname "the cyclone in calico."

Mary Bickerdyke (front row, center) on her 80th birthday, July 19, 1897, which was celebrated as "Mother Bickerdyke Day" in her home town of Bunker Hill, Kansas. More than 1,500 visitors came to pay homage to the selfless volunteer.

Mary Bickerdyke, the beloved volunteer nurse the soldiers called "mother."

Following the Battle of Belmont, Missouri, in November, Mrs. Bickerdyke was appointed matron of the new general hospital in Cairo by Gen. U.S. Grant, who liked the plucky woman's no-nonsense attitude. She subsequently followed Grant's troops to Fort Donelson, Shiloh, and Vicksburg on hospital ships and later accompanied Gen. William Tecumseh Sherman's forces overland to Chattanooga, Atlanta, and the Carolinas, riding part of the way on a captured Confederate horse. Wherever she went, Mother Bickerdyke added immeasurably to the wounded soldiers' comfort, seeing that they got hot baths and fresh bedding, clean cloth-ing, and nourishing food by hook or by crook. What she couldn't requisition from the government or the private U.S. Sanitary Commission, she improvised or just plain stole. The Sanitary Commission finally gave up trying to stop Mother Bickerdyke from filching supplies and made her an official agent in June 1862 so they could at least keep track of where their things were going!

The cyclone in calico had no patience for bureaucratic red tape where her boys were concerned and became known for her verbal assaults on uncooperative doctors. When one of these surgeons complained to General Sherman about her interference, the general, who particularly liked Mother Bickerdyke, told the doctor that he could do nothing for him as "she outranks me."

Mary ended the war by riding with General Sherman's troops in the Grand Review in Washington on May 24, 1865. In the years that followed, she continued her charitable work in Chicago and New York and in Kansas, where she settled in 1874. Mary Bickerdyke died at her home in Bunker Hill, Kansas, on November 8, 1901, and is buried in Galesburg, next to her husband Robert.

Philip Henry Sheridan   *1831 – 1888*

★ ★ ★ ★ ★ ★ ★ ★ ★ ★ ★ ★

No Northern general had as varied and successful a military career as Philip Sheridan. An accomplished infantry commander, Sheridan later became the Union's greatest cavalry leader and, with Sherman and Grant, one of the Army's most famous Civil War generals.

Philip Sheridan was born to Irish immigrant parents in Albany, New York, on March 6, 1831. When he was a child, Phil's family moved to Somerset, Ohio, where he received a limited education. Disappointed at missing out on the Mexican War because of his youth, he decided to pursue a military career and was admitted to West Point in 1848, when he was 17 (he lied about his age). Sheridan's volatile temper often got him in trouble at the Academy—in the worst instance he was suspended for a full year after attacking a cadet officer with a bayonet. In 1853, after five years, he finally graduated near the bottom of his class. Assigned to the 4th U.S. Infantry, he spent the next eight years as an undistinguished lieutenant fighting Indians in the Northwest.

With the coming of the Civil War, Sheridan finally received a promotion to captain on May 14, 1861, and was reassigned to the 13th U.S. Infantry in the Mississippi Valley, but he saw no service there. Toward the end of the year, he was appointed chief quartermaster in Gen. Henry Halleck's command, but this assignment did not last long. He was so displeased with holding a staff position that he made everyone's life miserable until he was named colonel of the 2nd Michigan Cavalry on May 25, 1862, and put in charge of a cavalry brigade in northern Mississippi.

(right) Sheridan in his favorite porkpie hat.

(opposite) Philip Sheridan, the commanding general of the Union's cavalry, on his favorite mount, Rienzi. Short, lightweight, and tough as nails, Sheridan embodied the ideal horse soldier.

Fort Larned, Kansas, one of the bases that Sheridan used as his headquarters while heading Army operations in the West after the Civil War.

The fight at Five Forks, Virginia, which finally broke the Confederate line at Petersburg, forcing the Army of Northern Virginia's flight to Appomattox Court House. A relentless fighter, Sheridan felt that Lee's retreating army should have been annihilated rather than permitted to surrender.

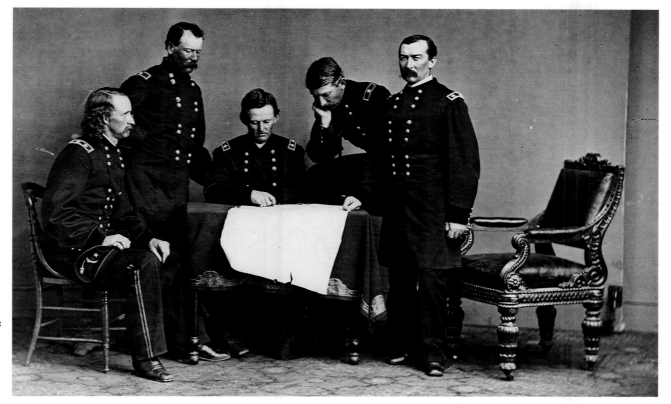

Philip Sheridan and his commanders at the end of the war. From left, they are Sheridan, George Crook, Wesley Merritt, James Forsyth, and George Armstrong Custer.

"Little Phil," as his men called him, first rose to prominence during the siege of Corinth, Mississippi. Attacking a Confederate infantry unit at Booneville on July 1, Sheridan reported that his dismounted troopers had inflicted heavy casualties on the rebels. Although his extravagant claims are now in doubt, Sheridan's victory at Booneville was hailed by his superiors and earned him a promotion to brigadier general and the command of an infantry division. Regardless of what really happened at Booneville, General Sheridan proved himself an unyielding fighter at the Battle of Stone's River, Tennessee, on December 31. Directing his division in a stubborn defense of the Union center, Little Phil held off three heavy assaults by Gen. Patrick Cleburne's troops while the rest of the Federal forces regrouped behind him. Following this engagement, he was promoted to major general and given command of a division in Gen. William Rosecrans's Army of the Cumberland.

Joining in Rosecrans's campaign against Gen. Braxton Bragg's Confederates in Tennessee the following year, Sheridan's division—like most of "Old Rosey's" troops— was driven off in a rout in the Battle of Chickamauga on September 20. But Little Phil redeemed himself at the Battle of Missionary Ridge on November 25, spearheading

Gen. George H. Thomas's attack against the seemingly impregnable Confederate center and forcing Bragg's troops from Chattanooga.

Sheridan's unremitting assault at Missionary Ridge earned him the respect of Gen. Ulysses S. Grant, at that time commander of the Union's war effort in the West. When Grant was promoted to general-in-chief in March 1864, he felt that Little Phil was the perfect man to command the Army of the Potomac's Cavalry Corps and had him transferred to that post on April 4. In one of his first engagements, at Yellow Tavern, Virginia, on May 11, Sheridan's horsemen succeeded in striking a major blow to Lee's cavalry when they killed Gen. Jeb Stuart.

In August, General Sheridan was ordered to clear Gen. Jubal Early's rebels from Virginia's Shenandoah Valley and to destroy the crops in that strategically important area, which served as the "breadbasket of the Confederacy." Advancing with more than 40,000 infantrymen and cavalry troopers, Sheridan defeated Early's forces at the Third Battle of Winchester on September 19 and at Fisher's Hill on the 22nd and then proceeded to lay waste to the valley's farmlands. Early launched a surprise counterattack at Cedar Creek on October 19 while Sheridan was 20

miles away in Winchester, and the Union troops were almost routed until Little Phil rode up and singlehandedly rallied his forces to achieve a decisive victory.

At the conclusion of the Shenandoah campaign, Sheridan joined the Union siege of Petersburg, Virginia. On April 1, 1865, he commanded the Federal attack at the Battle of Five Forks that successfully outflanked Robert E. Lee's defenses and forced the Confederate evacuation of Petersburg and Richmond. A week later, Sheridan's troops under Gen. George A. Custer succeeded in cutting off the Confederates' line of retreat at Appomattox Court House, forcing Lee to surrender to Grant on April 9.

After the war, Sheridan served as military governor of Louisiana for a few months, until his repressive administration forced even the radical reconstructionists to remove him. He was then assigned to the command of Army operations in the West, where his approach was summed up by his infamous assertion that "The only good Indian is a dead Indian." Sheridan was promoted to lieutenant general in 1869, and after Gen. William T. Sherman's death in 1884 was named to succeed him as general-in-chief with the rank of full general. Philip Sheridan died while on leave at Nonquitt, Massachusetts, on August 5, 1888.

Martin Robinson Delany   *1812 – 1885*

★ ★ ★ ★ ★ ★ ★ ★ ★ ★ ★ ★

Although slavery was one of the central issues of the Civil War, African-Americans were not permitted to play a major role in determining the outcome of the struggle. Most Northern whites, like most Southerners, harbored deep prejudices against blacks, whether slave or free. They did not feel that African-Americans could be trusted in combat, and it was not until 1863 that the Union permitted blacks to enlist; even then, they were segregated into units of "U.S. Colored Troops" and led almost entirely by white officers. A few black doctors were made surgeons, but only Maj. Martin Delany was commissioned as a field-grade infantry officer, becoming the highest-ranking African-American in the Civil War.

Martin Robinson Delany was born in Charles Town, Virginia (now West Virginia), on May 6, 1812, the son of free blacks Samuel and Pati Delany. He was named after his godfather, a local Baptist clergyman. When Martin was a boy the South prohibited both slaves and free blacks from learning to read or write. However, a kindhearted Yankee peddler passing through the area when Martin was six sold his mother a primer and secretly started teaching Martin and his brothers and sisters how to read. This surreptitious schooling continued for several years under a series of itinerant Northern merchants until the older children were able to instruct the younger ones, and the entire family became literate. When the authorities found out, they arrested Martin's mother, and after her release the Delanys moved to Chambersburg, Pennsylvania, where they could continue their education without fear of jail.

Martin was a hard-working, gifted student and in 1831 he left home to study with the Rev. Louis Woodson in Pittsburgh. Within

Dr. Martin Delany in his uniform as the first African-American infantry major.

five years he had learned enough to start studying medicine under a local doctor. After stopping to establish a newspaper in Pittsburgh and working with noted abolitionist Frederick Douglass on his magazine, *The North Star,* Martin was accepted to Harvard, completed his medical studies around 1852, and for several years practiced in Pittsburgh and Chatham, Ontario.

After leaving Canada for a trip to Africa and Europe, Delany returned to the United States in 1860. At the outbreak of the Civil War he proposed the establishment of a *Corps d'Afrique* composed entirely of African-Americans, but the idea was dismissed. Finally, in 1863, the Union Army agreed to accept black troops with the establishment of the famous 54th Massachusetts Volunteers. Dr. Delany served as a recruiting agent and examining surgeon for the unit in Chicago, but when he volunteered for appointment as the regiment's surgeon his application for a commission was turned down because of his race (the Army later accepted black doctors). Although deeply hurt, he continued to aid the Union cause by recruiting soldiers for black units in western Pennsylvania, New York, and Ohio. Dr. Delany never abandoned his plans for a corps of African-American troops, however, and in February 1865 he finally succeeded in placing a proposal before Abraham Lincoln that called for the raising of black troops to hold occupied areas of the South while more experienced white units continued offensive operations against the Confederate Army. Lincoln liked the idea and asked Dr. Delany if he would implement it; he agreed without hesitation, and on February 17 was commissioned the only black major in the U.S. Colored Troops.

Major Delany was detailed to the recently captured city of Charleston, South Carolina, where he was to recruit soldiers for his unit from among the city's freedmen. He arrived in Charleston just days before the end of the war, however, so he never achieved the goal of a *Corps d'Afrique* he had worked so hard to achieve. Martin remained in the Army, though, serving with the Freedmen's Bureau at Hilton Head, South Carolina, until 1868. Following his discharge, he stayed in South Carolina, serving as a trial justice and running for lieutenant governor on the Independent Republican ticket in 1874. Returning North after his defeat, Martin Delany died in Xenia, Ohio, on January 24, 1885.

John McAllister Schofield   1831 – 1906

★   ★   ★   ★   ★   ★   ★   ★   ★   ★   ★   ★

John Schofield had one of the longest, most distinguished careers of any of the North's generals. Having distinguished himself as a field commander during the war, he subsequently served as Secretary of War and finished his 46-year Army career as general-in-chief.

Schofield was born in Gerry, New York, on September 29, 1831, the son of Baptist minister James Schofield and Caroline McAllister Schofield. In 1843, he moved with his family to Freeport, Illinois, where he remained until 1849, when he was admitted to West Point. Schofield graduated seventh in his class in 1853 and was appointed to the artillery, serving in South Carolina and Florida. The intelligent young lieutenant was transferred to West Point as assistant professor of "natural philosophy" (i.e., science) in 1855, serving there until 1860, when he received a year's leave to teach physics at Washington University in St. Louis, Missouri.

At the start of the Civil War, Schofield offered his services to the divided state of Missouri and on April 26, 1861, was commissioned major of the 1st Missouri Infantry (Union), which he reorganized as a light artillery unit in June. He was later named chief of staff to Gen. Nathaniel Lyon, and assumed command of Lyon's battalion after the general was killed at the Battle of Wilson's Creek, Missouri, on August 10. The Union lost the battle, but Schofield's actions on the field, which helped save the Federal forces from disaster, earned him a promotion to brigadier general on November 21 and, in later years, a Congressional Medal of Honor.

General Schofield spent the following months organizing the Federal command in Missouri and combatting the state's guerrillas, rising to the rank of major general on May 12, 1863. In February 1864, he was appointed to command the Union's Army of the Ohio, leading the 23rd Corps throughout Gen. William T. Sherman's Atlanta cam-

(opposite) Gen. John Scofield during the Civil War.

paign that spring. Schofield distinguished himself at Kennesaw Mountain, where his troops broke through the Confederate defenses at Kolb's Hill, and at Atlanta, where he outflanked the Confederate line and forced the rebels to take refuge inside the city.

General Schofield's most important service during the war occurred after the fall of Atlanta in September. Gen. John Hood's Confederate force moved from the besieged city into Tennessee, hoping to draw Sherman's attention away from Georgia. Temporarily serving under Gen. George H. Thomas, Schofield directed his corps in an extended sparring match with the Southerners, inflicting heavy casualties on the opposing force at the Battle of Franklin on November 30 and aiding in Thomas's decisive victory over Hood at Nashville on December 15 and 16. Thereafter, Schofield and his men were transported to the North Carolina coast, where they occupied Wilmington and joined in Sherman's final campaign against Gen. Joseph E. Johnston's Confederates on March 23, 1865. When Johnston met to discuss surrender a few weeks later Schofield was one of Sherman's chief negotiators, helping to draft the terms which ended the war.

Nashville, Tennessee, the scene of Scofield and George Thomas's crushing victory over John Hood's rebels.

Scofield toward the end of his remarkable 46-year military career, when he was serving as general-in-chief of the Army.

After the surrender, General Schofield was sent on a secret diplomatic mission to France that resulted in the removal of the French troops supporting Emperor Maximilian in Mexico. Returning to the United States during the crisis over President Andrew Johnson's impeachment, Schofield was appointed Secretary of War on May 28, 1868, in place of the President's bitter enemy, Edwin Stanton. He served for the rest of Johnson's term of office, then resumed his army career as a major general. For the next 19 years, he commanded posts from New York to Hawaii. In the case of the latter, he was instrumental in the purchase of Pearl Harbor as a naval base. Following Gen. Philip H. Sheridan's death in 1888, Schofield was named general-in-chief of the Army and was subsequently promoted to lieutenant general. John Schofield retired from the Army in 1895 and died in St. Augustine, Florida, on March 4, 1906.

Joshua Lawrence Chamberlain 1828 – 1914

★ ★ ★ ★ ★ ★ ★ ★ ★ ★ ★ ★ ★ ★

It is usually impossible to attribute victory or defeat in a battle to a single turning point. Yet one could make a strong case for the determined stand of Col. Joshua Chamberlain and the 20th Maine Infantry, as having saved the Battle of Gettysburg for the North—and possibly the Union with it.

Joshua Chamberlain was born in Brewster, Maine, on September 8, 1828, to a military family: his great-grandfather had fought in the Revolution, his grandfather was a colonel in the War of 1812, and his father was a commander in the Maine border war with Canada in 1839. As a boy Joshua attended the military academy at Ellsworth, Maine, and then went on to Bowdoin College, graduating in 1852. He continued his studies at the Bangor Theological Seminary for three years, then was appointed an instructor in religious philosophy at Bowdoin in 1855. Within two years, the intelligent young man had risen to professor of rhetoric and modern languages.

When President Lincoln issued a call for volunteers in 1862, Chamberlain requested a leave from Bowdoin, ostensibly for study in Europe, but instead he enlisted in the Maine infantry. Joshua declined a colonel's commission, feeling that he was too inexperienced to command a regiment, but he accepted the post of lieutenant colonel of the 20th Maine Volunteers under Col. Adelbert Ames on August 8. They reported for duty in Washington, D.C., in early September, arriving just before the Battle of Antietam, where they were held in reserve.

Chamberlain's baptism of fire occurred at the Battle of Fredericksburg which followed in December 1862. Assaulting the fortified Confederate position on Marye's Heights late on the 13th, he and his unit were pinned down by enemy fire and forced to spend the night behind a small ridge facing the Confederate's infamous stone wall; Chamberlain later recalled that he covered himself with the corpses of Union soldiers to fend off the intense cold. The Maine regiment remained

Joshua Chamberlain, the Maine college professor turned Union general.

The summit of Little Round Top, the strategic high ground at Gettysburg saved for the Union by the unparalleled heroism of Chamberlain's 20th Maine Infantry.

at all costs, for if the Confederates were to dislodge his troops, they could mount a flank attack against the entire Army of the Potomac.

Chamberlain responded magnificently. Although his men were almost surrounded by Southerners, he led them in fighting off repeated Confederate assaults, holding the position against an overwhelming enemy force. Finally running low on ammunition, he ordered his troops to fix bayonets and charge, driving off the amazed rebels with hand-to-hand combat and saving Little Round Top—and the battle—for the Union.

After his action at Gettysburg, Chamberlain was assigned command of a brigade, but poor health forced him to go on extended leave in November 1863. Returning to duty in May 1864, he led his troops at Cold Harbor and Petersburg, where his bravery under fire on June 18 caused Gen. Ulysses S. Grant to award him a field promotion to brigadier general. After taking part in the Battle of Five Forks on April 1, 1865, General Chamberlain's troops joined in the pursuit of Lee's army to Appomattox Court House, where he was given the honor of accepting the surrender of the 28,000 soldiers of the Army of Northern Virginia on April 12.

Following the war, Chamberlain was elected governor of Maine. After serving four terms, he was appointed president of Bowdoin College in 1871, remaining on its staff until 1885. In 1893 he was awarded the Congressional Medal of Honor for his services at Gettysburg. Joshua Chamberlain died at Portland, Maine, on February 24, 1914.

trapped in this position throughout the following day, then covered the Union Army's retreat from Fredericksburg on the morning of the 15th, boldly holding a line just yards from the Confederate skirmishers.

Following the Battle of Chancellorsville in May 1863, Adelbert Ames was promoted to brigadier general and Chamberlain was appointed colonel of the 20th Maine Volunteers. At the battle of Gettysburg, he proved himself a truly extraordinary commander. The colonel and his regiment arrived on the battlefield on the afternoon of July 2, just after Gen. Gouverneur Warren became aware of the pressing need for the Union to secure Little Round Top. Chamberlain's regiment was immediately sent to the base of this pivotal promontory at the far left of the Union line and he was ordered—in the language of the time—to hold that ground

John Burns   1789 – 1872

★ ★ ★ ★ ★ ★ ★ ★ ★ ★ ★ ★ ★ ★ ★

The epic Battle of Gettysburg created dozens of heroes, including such famous generals as Lewis Armistead, George Pickett, Gouverneur Warren, and Daniel Sickles. But the most remarkable of Gettysburg's heroes was a 74-year-old cobbler named John Burns, the only civilian to fight among the 170,000 soldiers at the biggest battle of the war.

John Burns was born in Pennsylvania in 1789. As a young man he served in the War of 1812, seeing combat at Lundy's Lane. Later, he served as a town constable in Gettysburg, where he worked repairing shoes.

At the onset of the Civil War, John tried to enlist, but at 71 was too old for even the state reserves. Unable to fight for the Union, Burns served for a time as a wagon driver for the army in Washington, D.C.

When the Battle of Gettysburg began on the morning of July 1, 1863, Burns grabbed his old flintlock musket and left his home at the end of Chambers Street to do his part in repelling Gen. Robert E. Lee's invasion of the North. Marching over to McPherson's Ridge, the old man fell in with Col. Langhorne Wister's 150th Pennsylvania Infantry. Wister tried sending him to a protected spot in the woods but Burns insisted on staying in the open. The boys in the ranks laughed at him and called him "Daddy," but when they realized that he still knew how to shoot their jeers turned to respect.

After Colonel Wister's unit retreated, John fell in with part of the famous Iron Brigade. Taking part in some of the heaviest fighting of the day, Burns was struck three times, finally being disabled by a wound to his ankle. Dropping his musket and crawling to safety, the old soldier was captured and briefly detained by the advancing Confederates. Maintaining that he had been wounded while looking for a missing cow, he was treated by one of their doctors and released.

John Burns, the "old hero of Gettysburg," photographed by Matthew Brady a few days after the battle. **Behind him are his flintlock musket and the crutches necessitated by his wounds.**

When word of Burns's stand at Gettysburg spread after the battle, he was hailed as a hero throughout the North. Photographer Matthew Brady sought him out for his picture in mid-July, and when President Lincoln came to town that November to dedicate the National Cemetery, he specifically asked to meet the "Old Hero of Gettysburg." They later attended services at the Presbyterian church together; a plaque there commemorates the occasion.

John Burns died in Gettysburg on February 4, 1872. The memory of this colorful character has been kept alive by numerous authors including Bret Harte, who wrote a poem about him. The Old Hero of Gettysburg's role in the battle is commemorated today by a life-size statue of him, musket in hand, facing toward the enemy lines on McPherson's Ridge.

Andrew Hull Foote 1806 – 1863

★ ★ ★ ★ ★ ★ ★ ★ ★ ★ ★ ★ ★

At the very beginning of the Civil War, the Northern high command realized that the key to victory in the western theatre lay in that area's inland waterways. The rivers of the Mississippi Valley were the highways connecting the heartland of the Confederacy; if they could be secured for the Union, the areas adjoining them would fall. The man who did more than anyone else to win these waterways for the North was Flag Officer Andrew Foote, commander of the U.S. Navy gunboats on the upper Mississippi River.

Foote was born in New Haven, Connecticut, on September 12, 1806, the child of U.S. Senator Samuel Foot and Eudocia Hull Foot. As a boy Andrew—who later added an "e" to his family name—attended the Episcopal Academy at Cheshire, Connecticut, along with Gideon Welles, who would grow up to be wartime Secretary of the Navy. At the age of 16, Andrew was admitted to West Point but after a few months he left to become a midshipman. During his years at sea, Foote became a devout Christian and temperance advocate, doing away with daily grog rations and establishing the first "dry" ship in the Navy. After a tour of duty off the African coast in 1850, in which he captured an illegal slave ship, he also became a dedicated abolitionist, branding slavery a "revolting, filthy atrocity [which] might make the devil wonder."

Foote proved his mettle as a fighting man while commanding a small American fleet in Canton, China, in 1856. Assigned to protect American interests during the then-current Anglo-Chinese War, he led a party of 287 sailors and marines against the Cantonese coastal fortifications after his ships were fired upon, capturing four forts and 5,000 Chinese soldiers in three days.

Andrew Foote, the innovative U.S. Navy commander of the Northern Mississippi River.

Foote's gunboats running past Island Number 10 in April 1862. Here, as in many Civil War sieges, the Navy played a key role which has been largely overlooked in what was primarily a land war.

At the beginning of the American Civil War, Foote, by then a full commander, was superintendant of the Brooklyn Navy Yard. Promoted to captain in June 1861, he was transferred to Cairo, Illinois, in September and placed in charge of the new fleet of ironclad gunboats being assembled there. Raised to the rank of flag officer, he first took his gunboats into action during a joint campaign with Gen. Ulysses S. Grant's troops against Forts Henry and Donelson in February. Steaming up the Ohio River from Cairo to the nearby Tennessee River, Foote carried 15,000 of Grant's soldiers to a point just north of Fort Henry. The infantrymen were supposed to attack the garrison from the landward side while the gunboats shelled it from the river, but the muddy countryside delayed Grant's march and on February 6 Foote's guns pounded the fort into submission before the footsoldiers even got there. Since the cannons at Fort Henry inflicted minimal damage on the Union gunboats, this engagement demonstrated the strategic importance of ironclads for the first time in the war—a full month before the famous duel between U.S.S. *Monitor* and C.S.S. *Virginia* (formerly *Merrimack*).

On February 11, Foote's gunboats began steaming back up the Tennessee to join Grant in his assault on Fort Donelson, 12 miles east of Fort Henry on the Cumberland River. Three days later, they commenced their attack on the Confederate stronghold. But the defenses at Donelson proved much stronger than at Fort Henry, and Foote was unable to capture the position, leaving that to Grant's troops. During the attack, Foote's flagship, *St. Louis,* fell victim to the fort's guns. Its pilot house was badly hit, and the flag officer, who was seriously injured, had to return to Cairo before the end of the battle.

While recovering from his wounds, Foote turned his attention to a rebel fort on "Island Number 10" that blocked passage of the Mississippi River near New Madrid, Missouri. By lashing protective bales of hay to the sides of his gunboats and encasing his exposed pilot houses in an 18-inch-thick armor of chains and cables, the wily naval officer was able to send two of his ships safely past the fort's guns that April. Once beyond Island Number 10, the ships ferried Union troops to a strategic position below the fort, but the outpost surrendered without a fight on April 8, opening the entire northern Mississippi River to Federal traffic.

Foote's injuries forced him to step down from active duty in May. While on leave, he was promoted to rear admiral on July 16, 1862, in recognition of his superior service during the river campaigns. Before he could return to duty, Admiral Foote was stricken with a fatal disease and died in New York City on June 26, 1863.

George Brinton McClellan   1826 – 1885

★ ★ ★ ★ ★ ★ ★ ★ ★ ★ ★ ★ ★ ★

George McClellan was a study in contradictions. He was arrogant and self-confident most of the time—another general once described him as "the only man I ever knew who could strut sitting down"—yet he was doubt-ridden and timid in action. He was a commander who liked to see himself as a "Young Napoleon," yet he never won a single decisive victory. Despite these contradictions, however, he was indisputably a brilliant administrator and a gifted organizer who won his place among the heroes of the war by turning the raw recruits who streamed into Washington in 1861 into the force that eventually won the war in the East: the Army of the Potomac.

George McClellan was born in Philadelphia, Pennsylvania, on December 3, 1826, the son of Dr. George and Elizabeth Brinton McClellan. After studying at private schools in Philadelphia, he was admitted to the University of Pennsylvania in 1840 but left after two years to attend the U.S. Military Academy. McClellan graduated second in his class in 1846 and was assigned to the Corps of Engineers. Detailed for duty in the Mexican War, the young lieutenant served on Gen. Winfield Scott's staff, earning several commendations and learning the importance of a well-organized command structure.

After the war McClellan returned to West Point as an engineering instructor. He remained there until 1851, when he was assigned to surveying and construction projects in the West. Four years later he was transferred to the cavalry as a captain and sent to study the military systems of Europe. While there, he observed the siege of Sevastopol during the Crimean War, an operation that had a major influence on his tactics in the

(right) A Union artillery position at Fair Oaks, Virginia. **McClellan hoped to capture the Confederate capital with such siege guns in 1862, but he moved too slowly.**

(opposite) Gen. George McClellan, looking typically meticulous in his full dress uniform.

American war to come. Shortly after his return to the United States, Captain McClellan resigned his commission to become chief engineer of the Illinois Central Railroad. Within two years, he had risen to the presidency of the Ohio & Mississippi Railroad, headquartered in Cincinnati, Ohio.

At the onset of the Civil War, McClellan was appointed commander of Ohio's state troops on April 23, 1861. Three weeks later, on May 13, he was commissioned a major general in the U.S. Army and placed in charge of all operations between western Virginia and the Mississippi River. General McClellan came to national attention by defeating small rebel forces in western Virginia at the Battles of Rich Mountain and Corrick's Ford in mid-July. After the Union defeat at the First Battle of Bull Run on July 21, McClellan became the North's only successful general and was summoned to Washington, D.C., to take over command of the Union troops there. He embarked on an extensive program of training for both enlisted men and officers, successfully molding thousands of recruits into the well-disci-

plined soldiers of the Army of the Potomac, for which he was promoted to general-in-chief in November.

The men loved their charismatic commander, whom they affectionately called "Little Mac" and "Young Napoleon." Unfortunately, his rapid promotion and widespread popularity inflated McClellan's already large ego. He began thinking of himself as the unerring "savior of the Union" and resented any interference with his plans, particularly from the President, whom he regarded with contempt.

After months of training the North grew tired of waiting for McClellan to fight and, in spring 1862, President Lincoln—who described Little Mac as suffering from "the slows"—finally stripped him of his title as general-in-chief and ordered him into action. McClellan responded in early April by transporting 90,000 troops to the eastern tip of the Virginia Peninsula in a grandiose campaign to capture Richmond—a campaign that revealed all of Little Mac's weaknesses as a field commander. Convinced through faulty intelligence and his own fears that he was seriously outnumbered by Gen. Joseph E. Johnston's defending Confederates (when in reality he outmanned them almost two-to-

one)—McClellan moved slowly, planning a Sevastopol-like siege of the Confederate capital. After being held at Yorktown for a month by a small force of rebels, he reached the outskirts of Richmond in mid-May, six weeks after leaving Washington, D.C. Still, he could have easily stormed the city; instead, his men began digging in on a 15-mile siege line. When General Johnston attacked his forces at the Battle of Fair Oaks on May 31, McClellan was stunned; and when Gen. Robert E. Lee struck him in the first of the Seven Days' Battles at the end of June, the "Young Napoleon" rapidly retreated to a protected base southeast of Richmond on the James River. From there, the Army of the Potomac sailed back to Washington in early August, McClellan's Peninsular campaign having failed completely.

Soon after returning to Washington, Little Mac was detailed to stop Robert E. Lee's invasion into Maryland. At the Battle of Antietam on September 17, General McClellan committed his troops overcautiously, again permitting Lee's Army of Northern Virginia to hold off his much larger force. When McClellan subsequently allowed Lee's soldiers to escape into Virginia without pursuit, President Lincoln finally had enough of "the savior of the Union" and, on November 5, removed him from command.

Two years later a bitter McClellan ran against Lincoln as the Democratic nominee for President but was soundly defeated, carrying only three states. Afterward he was employed as an engineer and served as governor of New Jersey from 1878 to 1881. George McClellan died at Orange, New Jersey, on October 19, 1885.

The Army of the Potomac's retreat from Richmond during McClellan's Peninsular campaign. In evidence are the extensive baggage trains which slowed "Little Mac's" movements.

President Lincoln conferring with McClellan following the Battle of Antietam. Unable to get the general to move against Lee, Lincoln dismissed Little Mac a few days after this meeting.

Mary Edwards Walker *1832 – 1919*

★ ★ ★ ★ ★ ★ ★ ★ ★ ★ ★ ★ ★

Mary Walker is one of the most remarkable figures of the Civil War. One of the few female doctors in the country in 1861, she was the only woman to serve as an officer in the Union Army and the only lady to ever receive the Congressional Medal of Honor. 4Mary Edwards Walker was born in Oswego, New York, on November 26, 1832, the daughter of country doctor Alvah Walker. After attending a local seminary and teaching school for a few years Mary decided to follow in her father's footsteps, although it was very difficult for a woman to become a physician in the 1850s. Nevertheless, she was admitted to Syracuse Medical College in 1852 and received her M.D. with honors three years later. Following graduation, Dr. Walker married a classmate, Dr. Albert Miller, and they opened a joint practice in Rome, New York. The marriage was not a happy one, however, and they separated in 1859, divorcing ten years later.

After the separation Dr. Walker—who retained her maiden name—opened an office in Oswego. At the beginning of the Civil War in 1861 she traveled to Washington, D.C., to seek a commission as an Army surgeon. Although there was a serious shortage of doctors, she was quickly turned down because of her sex. Undaunted, she volunteered her services at the military hospital in the Old Patent Building while trying to get the surgeon general's office to reconsider her application.

Failing to get a commission in Washington, Dr. Walker enrolled in a new course of studies at the Hygeia Therapeutic College in New York, graduating on March 31, 1862. Later that year, she traveled to the headquarters of the Army of the Potomac in Virginia to once more seek a commission. She was rejected again but was permitted to remain with the Army as a volunteer physician. She

served in Virginia for several months and was of particular help after the bloody Battle of Fredericksburg in December.

In mid-1863 Dr. Walker headed south to Tennessee, where Gen. George H. Thomas hired her as a contract assistant surgeon for the 52nd Ohio Infantry with the rank of first lieutenant. Dr. Walker proudly donned a Union officer's uniform consisting of a modified frock coat and gold-trimmed trousers and was soon tending casualties from the Battle of Chickamauga in September.

Following the Battle of Chattanooga on November 23–25, Dr. Walker traveled around the local countryside treating civilians

Dr. Mary Walker, the only woman to serve as an officer in the Union Army, wearing the distinctive bloomer outfit which won her the title, "Little Lady in Pants."

and collecting intelligence for the Army. Caught by Confederate soldiers on April 15, 1864, she was imprisoned at Castle Thunder in Richmond until exchanged for a Confederate lieutenant on August 12, the first exchange ever of a female prisoner of war for a male of equal rank. After her release she was assigned as a doctor in the Military Prison in Louisville, Kentucky, and as director of the Orphan Asylum in Clarksville, Tennessee. Mustered out of government service in June 1865, Dr. Walker traveled to Washington, D.C., where she was the only woman to witness the hanging of the Lincoln assassination conspirators on July 7.

Mary Walker was awarded the Congressional Medal of Honor on November 11, 1865, for meritorious service as a doctor and intelligence officer. Thereafter she became a lecturer and advocate for women's rights. To bring attention to her belief in the equality of the sexes, she continued to wear men's clothing for the rest of her life, often appearing on the lecture platform in top hat and tails.

In 1917 Congress reviewed the list of Medal of Honor winners and stripped Mary (as well as 910 others) of her award. While protesting the decision, Dr. Walker fell in the Capitol building and died of her injuries on February 21, 1919. Mary Walker's Medal of Honor was finally reinstated in 1977, and her heroic role in the Civil War commemorated with a U.S. postage stamp in 1982.

Thomas Francis Meagher   1823 – 1867

★ ★ ★ ★ ★ ★ ★ ★ ★ ★ ★ ★ ★

The Civil War marked a major turning point for the North's Irish-Americans. Long the victims of anti-immigrant and anti-Catholic prejudices, they rendered loyal service to the Union during the war, service which helped them gain acceptance in Northern society. Tens of thousands of Irishmen fought in units from every state, but they were proudest of the famous Irish Brigade founded by Gaelic patriot Thomas F. Meagher.

Meagher (pronounced Mahr) was born in Waterford, Ireland, on August 23, 1823, the son of a wealthy politician and merchant, Thomas Meagher. After attending colleges in both Ireland and England, young Thomas became involved with the Irish nationalist movement and was arrested in Dublin for making a treasonous speech on July 11, 1848. He was initially condemned to death for his activities, but the sentence was commuted in July 1849 to banishment to Tasmania. Thomas escaped his exile in January 1852 by sailing to California. From there he traveled overland to New York City, becoming a U.S. citizen in August.

Meagher, a powerful speaker and natural leader, soon rose to prominence in New York's large Irish-American community. He lectured widely on his experiences, began studying law, and was admitted to the bar in 1855. The following year he became editor of New York's influential *Irish News*.

At the beginning of the Civil War, Meagher organized a company of Zouaves for the Irish-American 69th New York Militia. Commissioned the regiment's major on April 20, 1861, he proved himself a fearless fighter at the First Battle of Bull Run in July, remaining on the field even after his mount was shot out from under him.

When the 69th Militia's term of service expired in August, Meagher returned to

Meagher in his uniform as an officer of the 69th New York Zouave Company of the Militia (the "Fighting Irish") at the beginning of the war.

Meagher (on horseback, foreground) leading the Irish Brigade at the Battle of Fair Oaks, Virginia. The brigade carried the distinctive green flag seen here along with the Stars and Stripes.

Some of the hundreds of casualties that Meagher's brigade suffered at Antietam's Bloody Lane. Photographed a few days after the battle, this was one of the first pictures in history to depict the horrors of war first-hand.

The proud commander of the Irish Brigade, Gen. Thomas Meagher.

General Meagher led the brigade throughout the Peninsular and Second Bull Run campaigns later that year but did not have an opportunity to distinguish himself until the Battle of Antietam on September 17. There, he directed his troops in numerous assaults against the Confederates at the Bloody Lane. They experienced 60 percent casualties and earned a reputation as some of the toughest fighters in the Army of the Potomac. Meagher's greatest service to the Union, however, came at the Battle of Fredericksburg on December 13, when he boldly led the Irish Brigade on a virtually suicidal march against the masses of rebel riflemen entrenched on Marye's Heights. The unit was decimated, losing more than 500 men in a fruitless attack on the near-impregnable Confederate position.

Following his losses at Fredericksburg, General Meagher sought permission to recruit new volunteers for the brigade in New York but his request was repeatedly denied. Further casualties followed at the Battle of Chancellorsville on May 1–4, 1863. Thereafter, Meagher became disgusted with the Union high command and quit the Army. The general's resignation was not accepted, however, and on December 23 he was reassigned to Gen. William T. Sherman's command in Georgia. He remained at Savannah until discharged from duty on May 15, 1865.

After the war, Thomas F. Meagher served as acting governor of Montana Territory from 1865–1866. He died during an expedition on the Missouri River near Fort Benton, Montana, on July 1, 1867, when—reportedly drunk—he fell from a steamboat and drowned. His body was never recovered.

New York to recruit more Gaelic units. By early 1862 he had succeeded in raising three full regiments of volunteers—the 63rd, 69th, and 88th New York Infantry—which were organized into the Union Army's Irish Brigade (the unit later included the 28th Massachusetts and 116th Pennsylvania Infantry as well). Meagher was appointed the unit's commander and commissioned a brigadier general on February 3, 1862.

MAJOR GENERAL
Winfield Scott Hancock *1824 – 1886*

★　★　★　★　★　★　★　★　★　★　★　★　★

Few commanders in the Army of the Potomac could equal the record of Winfield Scott Hancock. An unflappable leader under fire, he played a major role in saving the Union forces at Chancellorsville and at Gettysburg, earning for himself the well-deserved title "Hancock the Superb."

Winfield Hancock was born in Montgomery Square, Pennsylvania, on February 14, 1824, and named after Gen. Winfield Scott, hero of the War of 1812. Young Hancock received his initial education at the Norristown Academy in Pennsylvania, where he displayed an early interest in the military by organizing a drill squad among his classmates. Admitted to West Point in 1840, Winfield graduated four years later at age 20, the youngest cadet in his class.

Hancock was commissioned a lieutenant in the 6th U.S. Infantry and assigned to duty in Texas. Two years later, he served under his namesake in the Mexican War, winning several commendations for gallantry. In the years that followed, Hancock was assigned to posts in Florida and in Kansas, where he saw further combat during the bloody clashes between the territory's pro- and antislavery factions in 1855.

At the beginning of the Civil War, Hancock, by then a captain, was quartermaster in Los Angeles, California, where he served under Lewis Armistead, a future Confederate general. After making his way cross-country, Captain Hancock was promoted to brigadier general and assigned command of a unit in the Army of the Potomac. Winfield first led his troops in Gen. George McClellan's Peninsular campaign the following year, serving with distinction in all of the Army's engagements through the Seven Days' Battles. At Antietam on September 17, General Hancock played a pivitol role in the assault at the Bloody Lane. Succeeding to command of the First Division of the Army's Second Corps after Gen. Israel Richardson was mortally wounded, he pressed the attack without

(above) Hancock (seated) with three leading division commanders at Gettysburg: Generals Francis Barlow (left), David Birney (center), and John Gibbon (right).

(opposite) An equestrian portrait that captures the elan of the general known as "Hancock the Superb."

hesitation, driving the rebels from the lane despite heavy losses. As a result, he was promoted to major general on November 29 and awarded permanent command of the division. Two weeks later, at the Battle of Fredericksburg, Virginia, Hancock's troops—particularly Thomas Meagher's Irish Brigade—spearheaded the second wave of attacks against the Confederate's position on Marye's Heights.

At the Battle of Chancellorsville, Virginia, the following spring, Hancock's men anchored the center of the Federal line. Hancock's leadership at this crucial position enabled the Army of the Potomac to avoid a total rout after Stonewall Jackson's daring flank attack on May 2. In the days that followed, he expertly covered the Yankees' retreat out of Chancellorsville and across the Rappahannock River. In recognition of his exemplary service at Chancellorsville, General Hancock was appointed commander of the Second Corps on May 22.

Winfield Scott Hancock's finest service to the Union occurred at the Battle of Gettysburg in July. After Gen. John Reynolds was killed on the first day of the fight, Union commander George Meade rushed Hancock to Gettysburg to take interim command. Arriving late on July 1, he approved Gen. Oliver Howard's selection of Cemetery Hill as the Union fallback position and spent the evening directing troop placements. The next day, while commanding the Army of the Potomac's left wing, he supervised the front's defense against Longstreet's flank attack. On July 3, the last day of the battle, he directed the repulse of Pickett's Charge, during which he was seriously wounded.

Congress subsequently voted its thanks to Hancock for his conspicuous action at Gettysburg.

General Hancock's wound kept him out of service for several months following the battle. Returning to duty at the end of the year, he led the 2nd Corps at the Battle of the Wilderness and at Spotsylvania, where it successfully broke through the rebel line at the "Mule Shoe" on May 12. Hancock's men repeated their success at the battle of Cold Harbor, Virginia, on June 3, the only troops to penetrate the Confederate breastworks in that battle.

During the siege of Petersburg which followed Cold Harbor, Hancock's wound opened up again and he was forced to resign command of the 2nd Corps on November 26, 1864. Transferred to Washington, D.C., he was ordered to raise a new Veterans Volunteer Corps composed of able-bodied discharged veterans (as opposed to the Veteran Reserve Corps, which was composed of invalid soldiers), but the unpopular program was soon abandoned. General Hancock finished the war as the director of the military department covering western Virginia.

After the war, Hancock remained in the Army, serving briefly as military governor of Louisiana and Texas until he was removed for being too lenient to satisfy the Radical Republican reconstructionists. He ran for President on the Democratic ticket in 1880, but was narrowly defeated by a fellow wartime general, James A. Garfield. Following this loss, Winfield Scott Hancock returned to duty at a military command on Governor's Island, New York, remaining at that assignment until his death on February 9, 1886. He is buried near his birthplace in Norristown, Pennsylvania.

James Birdseye McPherson   1828 – 1864

★ ★ ★ ★ ★ ★ ★ ★ ★ ★ ★ ★ ★ ★

James McPherson was regarded as one of the Union's finest generals. A brave and talented officer who rose from first lieutenant to major general in little over a year, his promising career was cut short by his death in action outside Atlanta.

McPherson was born near Clyde, Ohio, on November 14, 1828, the son of poor blacksmith William McPherson. When his father became disabled, 13-year-old James was forced to go to work in a local store to help support his family. The shopkeeper took an interest in the intelligent young man and, after sending him to the Norwalk Academy in Ohio for two years, secured his admission to West Point in 1849. McPherson graduated first in his class in 1853 and was appointed to the Corps of Engineers. He later served as an instructor at West Point for a year, then was assigned to surveying duties on seacoast fortifications.

The beginning of the war found McPherson stationed in San Francisco, California, along with Winfield Hancock and Lewis Armistead. Ordered to the East for duty, McPherson was promoted to lieutenant colonel on November 12, 1861 and was assigned as an aide to Gen. Henry Halleck, the Union commander in the western theatre of operations. In February 1862, McPherson was named chief engineer on Ulysses S. Grant's staff, accompanying the general to Fort Donelson and later to Shiloh, where he helped direct Grant's reinforcements on the first day of the battle. During the subsequent siege of Corinth, Mississippi, his troops thoroughly reconnoitered the area and handled themselves well, impressing Grant. McPherson was awarded his brigadier general's star on May 15. At the Battle of Corinth on October 4, General McPherson,

Gen. James McPherson, one of the finest Union commanders in the West.

still only a staff officer, took it upon himself to order an attack against Confederate General Van Dorn's retreating troops, earning himself a promotion to major general and a field command on October 8.

As the head of the Army's 17th Corps, McPherson played a leading role in Grant's Vicksburg campaign, which extended from the Battle of Port Gibson on May 1, 1863, through the Battle of Champion Hill on May 16. During the siege of Vicksburg which marked the culmination of the campaign, McPherson commanded the center of the Federal line opposite the battlefield's Great Redoubt. After the city surrendered on July 4, he was appointed military governor of the area.

When Gen. William T. Sherman was placed in charge of Federal operations in the West in March 1864, McPherson was awarded command of Sherman's Army of Tennessee. The 36-year-old bachelor requested time to marry his fiancée in Baltimore but Sherman refused, insisting that he needed McPherson immediately for his march against Atlanta. General McPherson followed orders and served with distinction through most of the campaign. On July 22, after arriving outside Atlanta, his troops were attacked by Gen. John Hood's Confederates while McPherson was away at Sherman's headquarters. Rushing to join his command, General McPherson accidentally rode into a Confederate patrol; displaying great elan, he calmly tipped his hat to the Southerners and tried to ride off—but was shot and killed. On hearing of his talented subordinate's death General Sherman wept, and later sent his fiancée a letter regretting that he hadn't allowed them time to marry. McPherson was subsequently buried in his home town of Clyde, Ohio.

(above) General McPherson (center, holding the compass) and two of his engineers at Vicksburg.

*(left) Part of the elaborate system of zig-zag trenches (called saps) that McPherson con-*structed at Vicksburg. **His troops had dug to within 15 feet of the Confederate defenses by the time the city surrendered.**

MAJOR GENERAL
Oliver Otis Howard 1830 – 1909

★　★　★　★　★　★　★　★　★　★　★　★　★　★

The North had few generals more dedicated to its cause during the Civil War than Oliver Howard. While Howard's personal record of bravery on the battlefield has suffered unfairly from his command's defeats at Chancellorsville and Gettysburg, he was a staunch Unionist and abolitionist who later headed the Freedmen's Bureau.

Oliver Howard was born on November 8, 1830, at Leeds, Maine, the son of a prosperous farmer, Roland Howard, and Eliza Otis Howard. After studying at the Monmouth Academy in North Hallowell, Maine, Oliver attended Bowdoin College, graduating in 1850. Accepted at West Point, he finished fourth in his class in 1854 and was appointed to the elite Ordnance Department. After serving at posts in New York and Florida, Howard returned to West Point in 1857 as instructor in mathematics.

At the beginning of the War Between the States, Oliver resigned his position at the U.S. Military Academy to accept a commission on June 4, 1861, as colonel of the 3rd Maine Infantry. He became a brigade commander later that month, and led his unit at the First Battle of Bull Run. In September, he was promoted to brigadier general.

General Howard first rose to prominence during the Peninsular campaign in 1862. He commanded his troops with distinction at the Battle of Yorktown on May 3 and was wounded twice in the Union defense at Fair Oaks on May 31, which resulted in the amputation of his right arm. Afterward, Gen. Philip Kearny, who had lost his left arm during the Mexican War, joked with him that the two of them could at least buy a pair of gloves together.

Howard returned to duty three months later, overseeing part of the Union Army's rear guard after the Second Battle of Bull

Howard, flagpole clutched beneath the stump of his right arm, attempts to rally his command following Stonewall Jackson's surprise attack at the Battle of Chancellorsville.

Run on August 30. At Antietam, Maryland, on September 17, he succeeded to the command of his division within the Army's 2nd Corps following the wounding of Gen. John Sedgwick during the devastating attack of Gen. Lafayette McLaws's Confederates in the West Wood. Howard succeeded in getting his badly shattered troops to safety at the northern end of the battlefield, earning promotion to major general on November 29. Two weeks later, at the bloody Battle of Fredericksburg, Virginia, Oliver again distinguished himself while attempting a flank attack against the Confederate line on Marye's Heights.

In recognition of his outstanding record of leadership, General Howard was awarded command of the Army's 11th Corps on April 2, 1863. The following month at the Battle of Chancellorsville, Virginia, that ill-fated unit was placed on the far right of the Union line, where it received the brunt of Stonewall Jackson's daring flank attack on May 2. Routed by the surprise assault, many of Howard's men ran for more than a mile to Gen. Winfield Hancock's position at the center of the Federal line, where Howard finally rallied them. Many soldiers, prejudiced against the predominantly German units in the 11th Corps, blamed the defeat at Chancellorsville on Howard's "Dutchmen," but most Union officers agreed with Gen. Darius Couch's assessment that "no corps in the army, surprised as the 11th was at this time, could have held its ground."

General Howard was also a major participant at the Battle of Gettysburg. He and his 11th Corps arrived on the field shortly after the beginning of the battle, around midday on July 1. Oliver, as the ranking officer on the spot, immediately assumed operational command of the Federal forces in place of Gen. John Reynolds, who had been killed, and deployed the 11th Corps to the north of

Brig. Gen. Oliver Howard (left), prior to the Peninsular campaign. He is pictured with a fellow officer from Maine, Lt. Col. Frederick Sewall.

town. In an unfortunate replay of Chancellorsville, Gen. Jubal Early's Confederates soon had Howard's corps outnumbered and outflanked, and the Yankees ran, causing the entire Federal line to disintegrate. Foreseeing such an emergency, as a good commander should, General Howard had designated Cemetery Hill, a high spot south of town, as a fallback position. There he formed the retreating Yankees into a strong defensive force, saving the Union Army from utter disaster and earning himself a vote of thanks by Congress.

General Howard and his 11th Corps were reassigned to Tennessee in September 1863 to assist the beleaguered Union garrison at Chattanooga. Following the Federal victory at the Battle of Missionary Ridge on November 25, Howard joined in Gen. William T. Sherman's Atlanta campaign, succeeding to command of the Army of the Tennessee

after Gen. James McPherson's death on July 22, 1864. Oliver continued to lead this force for the rest of the war, commanding Sherman's right wing during the March to the Sea and the campaign in the Carolinas.

At the end of the war, Howard was named head of the newly established Freedmen's Bureau, where he proved a dedicated administrator. During his term of office he founded the first college for African-Americans, which was named Howard University in his honor. General Howard subsequently served as superintendent of the U.S. Military Academy and as commander of the Military Department of the East, retiring in 1894. A year before he stepped down, he was awarded the Congressional Medal of Honor for his services at the Battle of Fair Oaks in 1862. Oliver Howard died at his home in Burlington, Vermont, on October 26, 1909.

The rout of the 11th Corps at Chancellorsville. Overrun by Jackson's rebels, Howard's troops unfairly bore the brunt of the blame for this Union defeat; the North had simply been out-generaled.

General Howard in later years, when he commanded the military operations in the eastern United States. He did not retire from the Army until 1894.

The statue honoring Oliver Howard on East Cemetery Hill, Gettysburg. The general's foresight saved this high ground as a Union fallback position on the first day of the fighting—and with it, the Army of the Potomac.

Clara Harlowe Barton   *1821 – 1912*

A t the beginning of the Civil War, the U.S. government had only minimal ability to care for its sick and wounded soldiers. The needs of these boys in blue were soon addressed by thousands of volunteer nurses and fundraisers, but no one served them with more dedication than Clara Barton, the little U.S. Patent Office clerk who went on to found the American Red Cross.

Clara, as she was always called, was born Clarissa Harlowe Barton on December 25, 1821, in Oxford, Massachusetts. As a young girl, she was painfully shy. The only hint of her future calling came when she nursed an invalid brother, hardly leaving his side during his two-year convalescence. At age 15, Clara became a schoolteacher to build up her self-confidence, and she spent the next 18 years instructing youths in one-room schools in Massachusetts and New Jersey. In 1854 she gave up teaching and moved to Washington, D.C., where she got a job as a copyist in the U.S. Patent Office.

When President Lincoln issued his call for troops in April 1861, one of the first units to respond was the 6th Massachusetts Militia, which included many of Miss Barton's former students. Visiting them in their temporary quarters in the U.S. Capitol, she was shocked to find that they had a shortage of food and lacked other vital supplies. Taking it upon herself to reverse the situation, she wrote to a host of people in Massachusetts seeking donations of food, blankets, and other creature comforts and was soon deluged with packages that she distributed to the boys. Thus her new career of service to the needy had begun.

After the First Battle of Bull Run, Miss Barton realized that her supplies were most needed at field hospitals near the battlefields and she set about getting them there. Acting entirely on her own, with no affiliation with the Army or its civilian aid group, the U.S. Sanitary Commission, she so impressed the

Clara Barton, dedicated Civil War nurse and founder of the American Red Cross.

surgeon general that he issued her a pass to travel with the Army "distributing comforts for the sick and wounded, and nursing them" in July 1862. From that time until the end of the war, Miss Barton was constantly in the field. She began at the Battle of Chantilly, Virginia, on September 1, where she was almost captured by advancing Confederates while tending to the wounded. Two weeks later, her supply wagons containing food and medicine began to arrive at the Battle of Antietam—the first to do so. They gave great comfort to the casualties of the war's bloodiest day of fighting.

The following spring, Miss Barton went South with a Union campaign on the South Carolina coast. She returned to Virginia a year later, in time to aid the wounded from the Battle of the Wilderness in May. Following that engagement, she joined Gen. Benjamin Butler's command at Bermuda Hundred,

where she was named superintendent of nurses—her only official Army appointment during the entire conflict.

After the war, Clara Barton spent four years overseeing a government program to identify and account for missing soldiers. Subsequently traveling to Europe for a rest, she became acquainted with the newly established International Red Cross organization and determined to see it established in the United States. Following a long campaign, the American Red Cross was established in 1882 with Miss Barton as president. She continued to serve as the organization's guiding spirit for 22 years, resigning in 1904. Clara Barton died at her home in Glen Echo, Maryland, on April 12, 1912.

John Fulton Reynolds   1820 – 1863

★ ★ ★ ★ ★ ★ ★ ★ ★ ★ ★ ★ ★

John Reynolds was one of the Union's finest field commanders. A fearless soldier, he died defending his native state at Gettysburg, just 50 miles from his birthplace.

John F. Reynolds was born in Lancaster, Pennsylvania, on September 20, 1820, the 13th child of Lancaster journalist and politician John Reynolds. After attending private academies in his native Pennsylvania Dutch country, young John was admitted to West Point in 1837. Upon his graduation four years later, he was commissioned a lieutenant in the 3rd U.S. Artillery and assigned to posts in the South.

During the Mexican War, Lieutenant Reynolds served under Gen. Zachary Taylor and earned commendations for bravery at the Battles of Monterey and Buena Vista. After the war he was posted to garrisons from New England to Oregon and in 1855 was promoted to captain. Five years later, in recognition of his exemplary service, Reynolds was appointed commandant of cadets and instructor in tactics at West Point by another Lancaster native and friend of the family, President James Buchanan.

With the onset of the Civil War, Captain Reynolds was commissioned lieutenant colonel of the 14th U.S. Infantry and assigned to recruiting duty. With the pressing need for good officers after the defeat at First Bull Run in July 1861, Reynolds was promoted to brigadier general and placed in command of a brigade of troops from his home state, the Pennsylvania Reserves. After serving briefly as military governor of Fredericksburg, Virginia, in May 1862, Reynolds and his command were transferred to the Virginia Peninsula to reinforce Gen. George B.

John Reynolds, the determined commander of the 1st Army Corps and one of the North's finest generals.

The death of General Reynolds at Gettysburg, July 1, 1863. **During the fighting at McPherson's Woods, he was mortally wounded by a Confederate sharpshooter.**

McClellan's Army outside Richmond. During the first of the Seven Days' Battles that ensued at the end of June, Reynolds led his troops with distinction, fighting off repeated assaults at Mechanicsville on the 26th and Gaines' Mill on the 27th.

On the night of June 27, while trying to check his lines in the dark, General Reynolds became separated from his brigade. The next morning he was captured. After several months in captivity, he was exchanged in August, shortly before the Second Battle of Bull Run. Reassigned to the command of his old division, he led a heroic counterattack against Gen. James Longstreet's Confederate force at Henry House Hill on the second day of Bull Run. During the Antietam campaign in September, he was detailed to organize the Pennsylvania militia by request of the state's governor and consequently missed the bloodiest day of the war. When he rejoined the Army of the Potomac in late September he was promoted to commander of the 1st Corps and commissioned a major general on November 29. Two weeks later, at the ill-fated Battle of Fredericksburg, one of his divisions under the command of George

Meade broke through the rebel line south of town, the only Federal unit to do so.

After Gen. Joseph Hooker's defeat at the Battle of Chancellorsville in May 1863, Reynolds was selected by President Lincoln as the next commander of the Army of the Potomac, but the general refused to accept the position unless Lincoln gave him complete guaranteed autonomy in running the Army. Lincoln refused and instead awarded the post

to George Meade. General Reynolds gallantly reassured his former subordinate that he bore him no ill will and indeed became one of Meade's most trusted commanders.

When Meade learned that Robert E. Lee's Army of Northern Virginia was nearing Gettysburg, Pennsylvania, on June 30, 1863, he dispatched Reynolds to the area with three corps—almost half the Army of the Potomac. On hearing that John Buford's cavalrymen had engaged James Archer's Confederates northwest of town on the morning of July 1, Reynolds led the First Corps to the troopers' assistance, urging his men into combat with the words "Forward! For God's sake forward!" During the ensuing engagement, Reynolds was mortally wounded by a Confederate sniper, the highest ranking officer on either side to die at Gettysburg. His body was carried to Lancaster and buried near his family home on July 4. The spot where John Reynolds was killed at the Gettysburg battlefield is now marked by an impressive equestrian statue of the general.

Henry House Hill, the scene of Reynolds's daring counterattack against James Longstreet's Confederates during the Second Battle of Bull Run.

Ulysses Simpson Grant   1822 – 1885

★ ★ ★ ★ ★ ★ ★ ★ ★ ★ ★ ★ ★ ★ ★

Early in the Civil War, Ulysses S. Grant seemed one of the least likely officers in the Union Army to achieve distinction on the battlefield. An uncharismatic, taciturn man who had trouble even getting a command, he gave no indication of being a good, much less great, general. Yet he went on to win some of the most decisive victories of the war, earning the rank of general-in-chief of the Union Army and exhibiting an utter determination which Abraham Lincoln summed up in just two words: "He fights."

The future general and U.S. President was born in Point Pleasant, Ohio, on April 27, 1822, and baptized Hiram Ulysses Grant. After working on his father's farm and tannery as a youth, Grant won appointment to West Point in 1839. Upon his arrival, he found his paperwork had been made out in the name of Ulysses Simpson Grant (Simpson being

his mother's maiden name) and, unable to get the error corrected, accepted his new name without complaint. Sam, as his classmates called him, (as in "Uncle Sam," from his initials), graduated in the middle of his class in 1843 and was assigned to the 4th U.S. Infantry in Missouri. After service in the Mexican War, where he was cited for bravery at Monterey and Mexico City, he married Julia Dent on August 22, 1848.

Following a two-year tour of duty on the Pacific Coast, and concerned about supporting his family on a captain's pay, Grant resigned from the Army in 1854 and sailed back east. Finding himself nearly penniless in New York, he borrowed money from a former West Point classmate, Simon Buckner, and returned to his family in St. Louis. There he unsuccessfully tried his hand at several occupations. After six rather unpro-

ductive years, he moved to Galena, Illinois, and took a job at his father's leather store.

At the beginning of the Civil War, Sam had a great deal of trouble securing a commission. He even appealed—unsuccessfully —to Gen. George McClellan for a position. But he was finally appointed colonel of the 21st Illinois Infantry on June 17, 1861. Detailed to Missouri, Grant was promoted to

(opposite) **The North's leading war hero, General "Unconditional Surrender" Grant, as he appeared during the Vicksburg campaign.**

(below) **Grant with a portion of his staff. Seated second from the right is Grant's military secretary, Lt. Col. Ely Parker, a full-blooded Seneca Indian from New York.**

President and Mrs. Lincoln's White House reception for Grant after his appointment as Lieutenant General.

brigadier general on July 31. Unfortunately, the new general's first fight proved to be a minor disaster. Attacking a small Confederate force at Belmont, Missouri, on November 7, Grant's undisciplined troops were driven off by reinforcements under Gen. Leonidas Polk—and Grant suffered his only defeat of the war.

Grant redeemed himself in February with a campaign which was to make him famous throughout the North. Moving out of Cairo, Illinois, in a joint offensive with Flag Officer Andrew Foote's gunboats, he quickly captured Fort Henry, the Confederate stronghold which controlled the lower Tennessee River, and then moved on Fort Donelson, which guarded the Cumberland River. After a sharp fight on February 15, Grant demanded and got "unconditional surrender" from the garri-

son's commander—Confederate Gen. Simon Buckner, ironically the man who had lent Grant that lifesaving money in New York years earlier. The victory earned Sam a new nickname, "Unconditional Surrender" Grant. A promotion to major general followed on February 16.

General Grant was assigned command of the Union forces in the Mississippi Valley. Soon, he began taking steps to secure the Mississippi River for the Union, and thereby divide the Confederacy in half. After beating back Gen. Albert S. Johnston's daring attack at Shiloh, Tennessee, on April 6 and 7, he began planning the capture of the last Confederate stronghold on the river, at Vicksburg, Mississippi. That campaign—Grant's most daring of the war—began in November when Sam marched his forces down the west bank of the Mississippi River past Vicksburg,

and then attacked the stronghold from the south, deep in enemy territory where he had no hope of reinforcement should he get into trouble. Demonstrating for the first time his true genius for field command, General Grant fought his way through Mississippi with minimal losses and, after a siege lasting a month and a half, captured Vicksburg on July 4, 1863. Following this significant victory, General Grant was placed in charge of the entire western theatre of the war, winning the battle of Chattanooga on November 25. This engagement convinced Abraham Lincoln that he had found the commander who would win him the war, and the President arranged Grant's appointment as general-in-chief of the Union forces with the rank of lieutenant general on March 2, 1864, thereby making Sam the first U.S. soldier of that rank since George Washington. The following spring, in his Virginia campaign of 1864, Grant attached himself to Gen. George Meade's Army of the Potomac to personally direct the effort against Robert E. Lee's Army of Northern Virginia. In a bloody war of attrition, Grant hammered away at Lee's forces at the Wilderness and Spotsylvania in May and Cold Harbor in June, knowing that the North could replace its heavy losses but the South could not. On June 18, Grant cornered Lee in the city of Petersburg, Virginia, and began the siege that finally ended the war. After ten months of constant pressure, Lee's Confederates abandoned the city on April 2, 1865, and seven days later were trapped at Appomattox Court House, Virginia, where Lee surrendered. Magnanimous in victory, Grant gave the Confederate commander generous terms, allowing his officers to retain their swords and the men to keep their horses for farm work.

"Unconditional Surrender" Grant became the North's leading war hero after Appomattox. A grateful nation made him its first full general in 1866 and then elected him President in 1868 and 1872. Unfortunately, Grant placed too much trust in undeserving friends and his administration was racked by scandal, none of which was his doing. After leaving office, the former President suffered severe financial losses and had to depend on a government pension and trust fund for income. Ulysses S. Grant died at his summer home at Mount McGregor, New York, on July 23, 1885, and is buried in the famous tomb bearing his name in New York City. Proceeds from his best-selling *Personal Memoirs,* published posthumously by Mark Twain's firm, Webster & Co., provided handsomely for his family after his death.

(above) *The first Federal wagons to enter the fallen city of Petersburg, Virginia, on April 3, 1865.* The city's surrender marked the successful conclusion of Grant's ten-month siege and the beginning of the end for the Confederacy.

(right) *Ulysses S. Grant as the 18th President of the United States.* Inexperienced in politics, he presided over an administration that was wracked by corruption.

James Samuel Wadsworth   1807 – 1864

★ ★ ★ ★ ★ ★ ★ ★ ★ ★ ★ ★ ★ ★ ★

James Wadsworth was a prominent Republican who ran for wartime governor of New York. But he was also a talented field commander who served the Union with valor from First Bull Run to the Wilderness.

Wadsworth was born to a wealthy family of Geneseo, New York, on October 30, 1807. He attended Harvard for two years, then turned to the study of law. Although he passed the bar he never practiced as an attorney, becoming preoccupied instead with the management of his family's extensive real estate holdings.

Wadsworth became involved in politics at an early age. Initially a Democrat, his abolitionist leanings led him to join the Free Soil party in 1848 and the Republican party after its establishment in 1856.

At the beginning of the War Between the States, Wadsworth turned down the offer of a major general's post from New York's Republican governor, feeling that he was too inexperienced for such a high rank. He did, however, accept appointment as an aide to Gen. Irwin McDowell, the Union Army commander at the First Battle of Bull Run. Impressed with Wadsworth's abilities, McDowell also recommended him for high command and he finally accepted a brigadier general's commission on August 9, 1861.

(left) General Wadsworth (seated, right) and his staff.

(opposite) James Wadsworth, the efficient New York politician turned general.

General Wadsworth was detailed to administrative and training duties until March 17, 1862, when he was placed in charge of the defenses of Washington, D.C. He was subsequently nominated as the Republican candidate for governor of New York, but he spent most of the campaign on duty in Washington and was defeated at the polls in November. Following the election he was appointed commander of the 1st Division, 1st Army Corps, a body that included such crack units as the Union's famous Iron Brigade and the 14th New York Militia. Members of the latter were called the "Red Legged Devils from Brooklyn" because of their distinctive red and blue uniforms. Although they did not see much action at the Battle of Chancellorsville in May 1863, Wadsworth's troops were the first Federal infantrymen to arrive at the Battle of Gettysburg on July 1. The general led his division in the heaviest fighting of the day at McPherson's Ridge and the Railroad Cut, where they held off the Confederate advance for hours, proving him to be a first-rate field commander as well as a talented administrator.

General Wadsworth's highly effective battlefield leadership was recognized during the Army of the Potomac's reorganization the following spring when he was one of the few nonprofessional soldiers retained in high command. As his 1st Division had been decimated in the fighting at Gettysburg, he was assigned a new division in the 5th Corps on March 25. While directing them in their first engagement at the Battle of the Wilderness on May 6, Wadsworth was shot from his horse and captured. Mortally wounded, James Wadsworth died in a Confederate field hospital on May 8, 1864; his body was later returned under a flag of truce and transported to Geneseo for burial. He was posthumously promoted to major general in honor of his superior service.

The fighting at the Wilderness, May 5–6, 1864. Wadsworth was mortally wounded leading his men there on the second day of the battle.

David Glasgow Farragut   1801 – 1870

★ ★ ★ ★ ★ ★ ★ ★ ★ ★ ★ ★ ★

During the War Between the States, naval forces played a much greater strategic role for the North than for the South. Unlike the Confederacy's defensive warfare, the Union's offensive campaigns constantly relied on ships for transporting troops, attacking rebel shore defenses, and closing Southern ports. The naval commander who was most successful in these operations was David Glasgow Farragut, one of America's greatest maritime heroes and the highest-ranking Hispanic in either the Army or Navy during the war.

David was born at Campbell's Station, Tennessee, on July 5, 1801. His father, George Farragut, was a native of the island of Minorca, Spain who served in the Russian Navy and then emigrated to America during the American Revolution, eventually settling in Tennessee. In 1807, George moved his family to New Orleans, and after his wife died the following year young David was kindly taken as a ward by David Porter, the U.S. Navy commander at New Orleans and father of David Dixon Porter. The commander arranged for Farragut to be named a midshipman at the incredibly young age of nine, beginning a naval career that would span 60 years.

After service in the War of 1812, Farragut was assigned to duty in the Mediterranean, where he learned to speak French, Italian, Spanish, and Arabic. Returning to the United States in 1821, he spent most of the next 40 years based at ports in the South, rising to the rank of captain in 1855.

At the beginning of the Civil War, Farragut was on leave at his home in Norfolk, Virginia. When that state seceded on April 19, 1861, the captain, an outspoken Unionist, moved his family to Hastings-on-Hudson,

(opposite) David Farragut, the hero of New Orleans and the U.S. Navy's first admiral.

(below) Farragut's flagship Hartford. The admiral was one of the few leading naval officers in the war to prefer old-fashioned wood-hulled ships like this one to the newer armor-plated gunboats.

New York, to await assignment. As a native Southerner, David's loyalties were initially suspect and he was only given shore duty in New York. However, a reassuring interview led the Navy Department to assign Farragut to command the strategically important blockade of the South's Gulf coast harbors on January 9, 1862, and he was promoted to flag officer.

Ordered to seize New Orleans, Farragut moved against the city in April. After bombarding its outer defenses for several days without effect, he decided to risk bypassing the guns to reach the city. On April 24, at 2 A.M., he gave the signal from his flagship, U.S.S. *Hartford,* and the Union squadron began steaming up the Mississippi River. Running the gauntlet of shore batteries, channel barriers, Confederate rams, and burning rafts designed to set his ships on fire, Farragut's fleet successfully arrived at New Orleans the next morning. The city, which was undefended, surrendered to Farragut on April 25, earning him a vote of

thanks by Congress and promotion to rear admiral effective July 16—the first American ever to hold that rank.

After securing New Orleans, the new admiral proceeded up the Mississippi River past Vicksburg, where he determined that the city could not be captured by gunboats alone, setting in motion Ulysses S. Grant's epic Vicksburg campaign. Farragut spent the rest of the year securing more Gulf ports, and by December the United States controlled the entire Gulf coast from Florida to Mexico with the single exception of Mobile, Alabama.

Following an unsuccessful attempt to capture Port Hudson, Mississippi, a Confederate stronghold controlling the Mississippi River between Vicksburg and New Orleans, Farragut sailed to New York for a rest. When he returned to the Gulf early in 1864, he organized an assault against Mobile Bay, Alabama, which he launched on August 5. After one of his lead ships was sunk by a torpedo (what we would call a mine today), Adm. Farragut gave his famous order to

Farragut's fleet steaming up the Mississippi River toward New Orleans on the morning of April 24, 1862. **The defending Confederates sent burning rafts downstream to ignite the Federal ships, but Farragut's sailors passed them without loss.**

"Damn the torpedoes" and proceed full speed ahead. After winning control of the bay on August 23, Farragut was promoted to vice admiral.

Health problems forced Admiral Farragut to go on leave after the Battle of Mobile Bay. He could not return to duty until January 1865, and then served only in a limited capacity in Virginia. After the close of the war, he was promoted to full admiral on July 26, 1866, and placed in charge of the Navy's European squadron. The admiral died at the Navy Yard in Portsmouth, New Hampshire, on August 14, 1870, and is buried in New York City.

William Alexander Hammond   1828 – 1900

★ ★ ★ ★ ★ ★ ★ ★ ★ ★ ★ ★ ★ ★

In April 1861, the U.S. Army was totally unprepared to deal with the hundreds of thousands of sick and wounded soldiers that the Civil War would generate. Its entire Medical Department consisted of only 114 doctors and one hospital, supervised by an aging surgeon general who was more concerned with saving money than saving lives. The task of organizing a medical department which could meet the war's needs fell to Dr. William Hammond, the brilliant physician and administrator who was appointed surgeon general in 1862.

Hammond was born in Annapolis, Maryland, on August 28, 1828, the son of Dr. John Hammond. He received his basic schooling in Harrisburg, Pennsylvania, and then studied medicine at the University of the City of New York (now NYU), graduating in 1848. After a year of further training at the Pennsylvania Hospital in Philadelphia, he applied for a medical post in the Army and was appointed an assistant surgeon with the rank of lieutenant. Dr. Hammond spent the next ten years at garrisons throughout the United States, including a tour of duty at West Point. He resigned his commission in 1859 to become professor of anatomy and physiology at the University of Maryland at Baltimore.

With the onset of the Civil War, Dr. Hammond left his prestigious position at the university to reenlist in the Army Medical Department. In a shortsighted move, typical of the Medical Department early in the war, Hammond's previous service was discounted and he was commissioned a junior assistant surgeon without any seniority, just like every other doctor entering the Army. After organizing a hospital in Baltimore, Dr. Hammond was assigned as medical inspector with the Union forces in western Virginia. His careful work in the camps and field hospitals there brought him to the attention of the U.S. Sanitary Commission, a private relief agency which functioned much like

today's Red Cross. When the office of surgeon general subsequently became vacant on April 14, 1862, the highly influential officials of the Sanitary Commission lobbied to have Dr. Hammond appointed to the position, appealing directly to President Lincoln when Secretary of War Edwin Stanton refused to consider their candidate. With Lincoln's backing, Hammond was named Surgeon General on April 25 and promoted from lieutenant to brigadier general, a move that pleased his backers but made enemies of Stanton and many of the doctors he bypassed.

The new surgeon general quickly set about making improvements in his department. He increased both the number and quality of physicians in the service, offering better pay to entice doctors to enlist while making the entrance examination for surgeons more demanding. He directed the construction of more than 150 hospitals for wounded soldiers throughout the North, established Army pharmaceutical labs for the production of medicines, and authored a manual for the

use of his doctors. Most importantly to the boys in blue, Surgeon General Hammond supervised the development of an efficient system of ambulances and field hospitals which vastly improved their treatment after battle. In addition to these practical advances, Dr. Hammond, a farsighted researcher, ordered his surgeons to keep detailed records of their cases, laying the groundwork for the department's massive 6,000-page *Medical and Surgical History of the War of the Rebellion*, and directed them to send noteworthy study specimens—such as Gen. Daniel Sickles's shattered leg bones—to Washington for an Army Medical Museum that is still in existence.

Not all of Dr. Hammond's changes were well received by the Army, and he often came into conflict with Secretary of War Stanton, who felt that the surgeon general exercised too much autonomy. In July 1863, Stanton, urged on by some of the surgeons Hammond had superseded, mounted an investigation of the medical department that resulted in Hammond's dismissal on flimsy charges on August 18, 1864. Following this he returned to private practice, becoming a noted neurologist in New York. He succeeded in having his dismissal overturned in 1879 and was restored to the rank of brigadier general, retired. After serving as a professor at several medical schools, William Hammond eventually moved to Washington, D.C., where he died on January 5, 1900.

Philip Kearny   1815 – 1862

★ ★ ★ ★ ★ ★ ★ ★ ★ ★ ★ ★ ★ ★ ★

Philip Kearny (pronounced Carney) was probably the most colorful officer in the Union Army, and certainly one of its best fighters. Affluent and well educated, he was a born soldier who fought on three continents and boasted that he could "make men follow me to hell."

Kearny was born in New York City on June 2, 1815, the son of Philip and Susan Watts Kearny. When his mother died in 1823, young Phil was raised by her father, John Watts, Jr., a member of one of New York's most prominent families. After attending several private boarding schools, Phil hoped to follow in the footsteps of his uncle, Gen. Stephen Watts Kearny, and enter into a military career, but his grandfather would not permit him to apply for admission to West Point. Kearny decided to study law instead—after turning down his grandfather's offer of $1,500 a year (then a significant sum) if he would enter the ministry. He received his law degree from Columbia College in 1833.

On his grandfather's death in 1836, Kearny inherited almost a million dollars. Despite his new-found wealth, he quickly applied for a commission in the U.S. Army and was appointed a second lieutenant in the 1st Dragoons on March 8, 1837. After two years' service on the frontier, Kearny was sent to study tactics at the French Cavalry School at Saumur and served in Algiers with the French Chasseurs. On returning to the United States, he served as aide-de-camp to two successive generals-in-chief, Alexander Macomb and Winfield Scott. During the Mexican War Kearny was reappointed to the Dragoons, commanding General Scott's personal guard. While leading a charge at Churubusco, he was severely wounded, resulting in the subsequent ampu-

General Kearny, one of the North's finest officers, at the beginning of the Civil War.

Kearny's death during the battle of Chantilly, Virginia, on September 1, 1862. He rode with the reins in his mouth so his single arm would remain free.

The battle of Williamsburg, Virginia, where Kearny first led his command into combat.

tation of his left arm. Thereafter, he rode with the reins in his mouth during combat so that his right hand could be free to wield a saber.

After subsequent service in California, Kearny resigned from the Army in 1851, eventually purchasing an estate near Newark, New Jersey, in an area which has since been named Kearny in his honor. In 1859, the adventuresome soldier traveled to France to serve with the Imperial Guard's Cavalry in the Italian War, winning the Cross of the Legion of Honor at the Battle of Solferino.

At the onset of the Civil War, Kearny returned to the United States to seek a command. Commissioned a brigadier general on August 7, 1861, he was assigned a brigade of troops from his home state of New Jersey.

While taking part in McClellan's Peninsular campaign the following year, Kearny was given command of a division in the Army's 3rd Corps on April 30. Five days later, he led his command in combat at the Battle of Williamsburg. Pursuing Gen. Joseph E. Johnston's retreating Confederates in the aftermath of the battle, he found his path blocked by an Army wagon train. The hard-bitten soldier reacted typically, threatening to "set the torch to your goddamned cowardly wagons." He finally got past the tangle, and his troops performed with distinction against the South's rear guard, inflicting heavy casualties. Kearny continued to serve with conspicuous bravery throughout the campaign, and was rewarded with a promotion to major general on July 4.

During one of the actions on the Peninsula, Kearny accidently chewed out an officer

from another command, mistaking the man for one of his subordinates. To avoid such mistakes in the future, the general ordered all of his officers to wear a lozenge-shaped red patch on their caps so they could be easily distinguished. These "Kearny patches" soon became a point of pride for his division and were adopted by the whole command. Following Kearny's example, the entire U.S. Army subsequently adopted a series of division and corps badges, which were the forerunners of the modern service's shoulder patches.

Following the Peninsular campaign, Kearny's troops played a conspicuous role at the Second Battle of Bull Run on August 29 and 30. On the first day of the fight, his troops almost broke through Gen. A. P. Hill's line on the Confederate left, but for the arrival of rebel reinforcements. During the Southerners' counterattack the next day, Kearny's division held its ground on Henry House Hill while the rest of the Union Army retreated, almost the only Yankees to avoid a rout that afternoon.

On September 1, Confederate troops caught up with the retreating Federal forces at Chantilly, Virginia. While reconnoitering the area during the subsequent battle, General Kearny accidently rode behind the rebel lines and was shot to death while trying to escape capture. His body and sword were returned under a flag of truce by order of Robert E. Lee, and the man whom General Scott described as "the bravest man I ever knew, and a perfect soldier" was buried in his family vault in New York City's Trinity Episcopal Church. In 1912 Philip Kearny was reinterred at Arlington National Cemetery, where the State of New Jersey has erected an impressive monument in his honor.

Edwin McMasters Stanton *1814 – 1869*

On the surface, Edwin Stanton hardly fit the mold of a great wartime leader. A humorless, self-serving lawyer, he had nothing but contempt for Abraham Lincoln before the war, once even labeling him "the original gorilla." But he was a brilliant administrator and, after his appointment as Secretary of War in 1862, worked tirelessly toward victory, doing more than any government official except Lincoln to win the struggle for the North.

Edwin Stanton was born in Steubenville, Ohio, on December 19, 1814, the son of Dr. David Stanton. Raised in a Quaker household, Edwin was brought up as a strict abolitionist; and although the future secretary of war became a Methodist, forgoing Quaker belief in pacifism, he never lost his anti-slavery fervor.

When Dr. Stanton died in 1827, Edwin was forced to leave school and get a job. After working in a bookstore for a few years, he saved up enough money to enter Kenyon College in 1831. Forced to withdraw in his junior year due to lack of funds, he subsequently began studying law under a local attorney.

After passing the bar in 1836, Stanton rapidly developed a successful practice and moved to Pittsburgh, Pennsylvania. As his reputation as a lawyer grew, he received many important cases, among them an 1856 patent suit involving the McCormick reaper. During this trial he was assigned as cocounsel a lanky Illinois lawyer named Abraham Lincoln, who developed quite a respect for Stanton's legal expertise even though he was constantly insulted by the arrogant Pennsylvania barrister. In the years that followed, Stanton came to national attention by successfully representing the United States in a

The North's irascible secretary of war, Edwin Stanton. Although he was contemptuous of Abraham Lincoln personally, he was nevertheless a highly effective member of the President's cabinet.

Stanton's office in the War Department. **An elaborate system of field telegraph lines kept the secretary informed of developments on all fronts.**

California land title case involving more than $150 million in property and by defending Congressman Daniel Sickles in his spectacular 1859 murder trial. By 1860 Stanton was recognized as the nation's leading lawyer and, although not previously involved in politics, he was appointed attorney general on December 20, to serve through the last months of President Buchanan's administration. After Abraham Lincoln took office in March 1861, Stanton returned to private practice in Washington, D.C.

Various explanations have been suggested as to just how Stanton, an anti-Lincoln Democrat with no military experience, came to be appointed head of Lincoln's War Department. The President's first war secretary, a political appointee named Simon Cameron, proved incompetent and the War Department was wracked with graft. Lincoln, it would seem, named Stanton as Cameron's successor on January 15, 1862, for several reasons: first, despite his political affiliation, Edwin was a staunch Unionist who, in Lincoln's opinion, would see the war through to victory; second, he was recommended by such luminaries as Secretary of State William H. Seward and Gen. George B. McClellan, whom he had advised as an attorney; third, he was a Pennsylvanian, as was Cameron, and would therefore fulfill the President's political promise to give a cabinet post to someone from that state; and, most importantly, the brilliant attorney had thoroughly impressed Lincoln with his abilities during the McCormick case and the President was willing to overlook their personal differences for the sake of the war effort.

The War Department building in Washington, D.C., nerve center of the Federal war effort. President Lincoln often spent hours here with Stanton reviewing dispatches from the front.

The hanging of Lincoln's assassination conspirators on July 7, 1865. Stanton pursued the assassination investigation without stop until he was satisfied that all those involved had been apprehended and punished.

THE SCAPE-GOAT NOW ON EXHIBITION IN WASHINGTON.

Stanton as scapegoat—a cartoon from **Harper's Weekly** *of July 19, 1862.* **The secretary of war was widely blamed for the Union's failures during the first years of the war.**

Secretary Stanton immediately set about improving the War Department, weeding out corrupt employees and demanding quality supplies instead of the shoddy merchandise and spoiled food that the government had been receiving from private vendors. He was ruthless in his prosecution of the war, authorizing illegal arrests of civilians, turning on his former friend George McClellan when the general proved too slow, and even overriding President Lincoln's requests on war matters. But he got things done when no one else could. His reinforcement of the Federal garrison at Chattanooga, Tennessee, following the Battle of Chickamauga in Sep-

tember 1863—transporting 23,000 troops from as far away as Mississippi and Pennsylvania in just seven days—stands as one of the most incredible feats of the war.

Stanton was clearly the most powerful member of Lincoln's cabinet. After the President's assassination on April 14, 1865, he assumed almost dictatorial powers over the executive branch, overshadowing even the new President, Andrew Johnson. Merciless in his pursuit of the assassination conspirators, Stanton began his investigation before Lincoln had even died and carried it through until John Wilkes Booth was killed and his fellow conspirators hanged. His insistence on secrecy, keeping the suspects isolated with their heads covered by heavy canvas hoods, has led to wild accusations that Stanton was trying to keep them from revealing his own role in the assassination, but there is absolutely no evidence linking him with the President's murder.

Stanton was retained as war secretary during the Johnson administration, allying himself with the Radical Republicans and causing Johnson much trouble over the issue of Reconstruction. When Johnson dismissed Stanton on February 21, 1868, in violation of the Tenure of Office Act (later held to be unconstitutional), the action was cited as the grounds for Johnson's impeachment. During the President's trial Stanton refused to vacate his office, living in the War Department and posting an armed guard outside the building to prevent his removal, but when Johnson was declared innocent on May 26 Stanton knew he was beaten and resigned. The cabinet post then passed to Civil War hero John Schofield.

Following an extended rest, Stanton returned to the practice of law. After Ulysses S. Grant's inauguration as President in 1869, Edwin Stanton achieved his lifelong ambition—he was appointed to the U.S. Supreme Court. But he never served on the Court, dying at his home in Washington just four days later, on December 24, 1869.

Benjamin Mayberry Prentiss   1819 – 1901

★ ★ ★ ★ ★ ★ ★ ★ ★ ★ ★ ★

The Battle of Shiloh in April 1862 was one of the Civil War's most decisive engagements, a major turning point for the war in the West. The battle might well have been a Federal rout had Gen. Benjamin Prentiss not led a determined stand that bought the Union Army enough time to regroup and win the battle the following day.

Prentiss was born to old-line Yankee parents in Belleville, western Virginia, on November 12, 1819. After studying at a military school in Virginia, Benjamin moved west with his family in 1836, finally settling in Illinois in 1841. During the Mexican War he served as a captain in the 1st Illinois Volunteers and distinguished himself at the Battle of Buena Vista. Afterward he returned to Illinois to study law, becoming a successful attorney.

When the Civil War broke out in April 1861, Prentiss was serving as a colonel in the Illinois militia. Assigned to Cairo, at the confluence of the Mississippi and Ohio Rivers, he soon earned a name for himself by capturing two steamboats heading South with munitions on two successive days, April 24 and 25. A few days later he was named colonel of the 10th Illinois Infantry, and by

Benjamin Prentiss, Union hero, at the Battle of Shiloh.

August he was promoted to brigadier general, with responsibility for Union operations in central and northern Missouri.

In early 1862, General Prentiss was ordered to take command of a division within the Federal army that Ulysses S. Grant was

gathering near Shiloh, Tennessee. On April 6, just five days after he reported for duty, Confederate Gen. Albert S. Johnston launched a sneak attack against Grant's soldiers at Shiloh, swinging in from the southwest at dawn and quickly driving back the surprised Yankees. Later that morning General Prentiss rallied his command at a densely wooded high ground near the center of the battlefield, and held off a dozen rebel assaults in heavy fighting that earned the spot its name, "the Hornets' Nest." The Confederates then ringed the position with 62 artillery pieces and Prentiss endured a two-hour bombardment, but he was finally forced to surrender around 5:30 in the afternoon. Still, the six hours that he had held the Hornets' Nest gave Grant time to establish a fallback position at the northeast corner of the battlefield and save his army from defeat.

Benjamin Prentiss was held as a Confederate prisoner until exchanged in October. After his release, he was assigned command of the Union forces in eastern Arkansas, where he decisively defeated a Confederate force under Gen. Theophilus Holmes on July 4, 1863. Although he had been promoted to major general the previous March 13, he resigned from the Army on October 28, feeling that he had been purposely sidelined from the war by his assignment to Arkansas. Returning to Illinois, Prentiss resumed his law practice. After the war he moved to Missouri, where he worked as an attorney and land agent. Benjamin Prentiss died at Bethany, Missouri, on February 8, 1901.

The action at the Hornets' Nest midday on April 6, 1862. **Prentiss can be seen directing the Union defense on horseback to the right.**

Ephraim Elmer Ellsworth   *1837 – 1861*

★ ★ ★ ★ ★ ★ ★ ★ ★ ★ ★ ★

President Lincoln's call for troops at the beginning of the Civil War led to the formation of a wide variety of volunteer units including Scotsmen in kilts and lumberjacks in red flannel shirts, but none were more popular than the Union's colorful Zouave regiments. Based on a crack French Algerian unit, the American Zouaves were usually outfitted in distinctive Arab-style uniforms that included baggy pantaloons, turbans, and sashes. These exotic troops, which added so much to the martial spirit of the North at the beginning of the war, were popularized in the United States by the young man who became the first Union officer to die in the War Between the States, Elmer Ellsworth.

Ephraim Elmer Ellsworth was born in Malta, New York, on April 11, 1837, the son of Ephraim and Phoebe Ellsworth. As a boy, Elmer (as he preferred to be called) hoped to enter West Point, but his limited public school education was insufficient for him to pass the entrance examinations. Leaving Malta as a teenager, he moved to New York City and then Chicago, where he was employed as a law clerk and patent solicitor.

While in Chicago, Elmer learned about the Zouaves from his French fencing coach. He became fascinated by the colorful soldiers, reading everything he could about them, even sending to France for their drill manuals. In April 1859, he organized the first American Zouave unit, the U.S. Zouave Cadets. Like their Algerian counterparts, Ellsworth's Zouaves were uniformed in red trousers, short blue jackets, and broad red sashes, and they practiced the French Zouaves' complex drill, which took over four hours to perform completely. Ellsworth's Zouaves soon developed into the finest drill team in the country, and during an exhibi-

Elmer Ellsworth, the first Union officer to die in the Civil War. He is seen here in his uniform as colonel of the Fire Zouaves.

tion tour through the Northeast in the summer of 1860, they inspired the creation of dozens of other Zouave units that fought during the Civil War, including New York's famed Duryée's Zouaves.

On returning from his tour, Elmer became a clerk in Abraham Lincoln's law office in Springfield, Illinois, studying law and assisting with Lincoln's Presidential campaign. After Lincoln's election, Ellsworth accompanied the President-elect to Washington, hoping to establish a government militia bureau. Following the Federal declaration of war on April 15, 1861, however, Elmer returned to his native state to raise a command. Within days Ellsworth had recruited and equipped an entire Zouave regiment from the ranks of New York City's fire companies —the 1st New York Fire Zouaves—and was commissioned its colonel. The Fire Zouaves arrived in Washington, D.C., on April 29, one of the first Federal units to answer the President's call for troops. The jaunty soldiers and their famous commander quickly became local favorites, particularly after they helped put out a fire at Washington's leading hotel, Willard's.

The death of Ellsworth in the Marshall House Hotel, Alexandria, Virginia. **Col. Ellsworth is shown descending the staircase, flag in hand, as innkeeper James Jackson (*right*) shoots him despite Francis Brownell's unsuccessful attempt to divert Jackson's gun.**

Colonel Ellsworth and his Zouaves remained in the capital until May 24, when they were detailed to sail down the Potomac and secure Alexandria, Virginia, for the Union. On entering the city, Ellsworth spotted a Confederate flag flying from the Marshall House Hotel. With typical enthusiasm Elmer decided to remove the colors himself, and while coming down the stairs he was mortally wounded by a shotgun blast fired by the hotel's proprietor, James T. Jackson. Jackson was immediately killed by Private Francis Brownell, who had accompanied Ellsworth to the hotel; Brownell was subsequently awarded the Congressional Medal of Honor for his action.

The Fire Zouaves leaving New York on April 29, 1861. **The hastily assembled regiment had fairly sedate gray and black uniforms; the colorful Arabian-styled outfits typical of most Zouave companies were too ornate to be produced within the week-and-a-half that it took Ellsworth to raise his unit.**

Elmer Ellsworth was hailed as a Union martyr, and his death was mourned throughout the North. Lincoln had his friend's body laid in state in the White House and then sent to New York by special train. Following memorial services at New York City and Albany, Elmer Ellsworth was buried in Mechanicville, New York, near his boyhood home.

William Tecumseh Sherman 1820 – 1891

★ ★ ★ ★ ★ ★ ★ ★ ★ ★ ★ ★ ★

While the North and South both had their share of talented commanders, there were few military geniuses among them; William Tecumseh Sherman, the Union's greatest tactician, was one. The commander who proved that "War is hell" with his March to the Sea developed the modern concept of "total warfare," for the first time putting into rigorous practice the theory that military victory must be linked to the destruction of the enemy population's ability to wage war.

The future general was born in Lancaster, Ohio, on February 8, 1820, one of 11 children of prominent jurist Charles Sherman,

who named him after the famous Indian leader. After his father's death in 1829 "Cump," as his family called him, was raised by local attorney Thomas Ewing, who gave him the first name William (Sherman later married Ewing's daughter Ellen). With Mr. Ewing's assistance, Cump was admitted to West Point in 1836. Graduating sixth in his class four years later, he was commissioned a lieutenant in the 3rd U.S. Artillery and served at posts in the South until the outbreak of the Mexican War, when he was assigned to staff duties in California. After subsequent service in Washington, D.C.,

Sherman resigned his commission on September 6, 1853, to become a banker in San Francisco. When the bank failed in 1857, he briefly tried his hand at law, losing the only case he brought to court, and then became superintendent of a military academy in

(opposite) **William Tecumseh Sherman, the general who waged total warfare against the South.**

(below) **The 19th U.S. Infantry storming the Confederate trenches along Sherman's front at Vicksburg.** **Although his men were later forced to retreat back to the Union lines, Sherman proudly ordered them to emblazon "First at Vicksburg" on their regimental colors.**

Sherman's generals during the March to the Sea.
From left: Oliver Howard, John Logan, William Hazen, Sherman, Jefferson C. Davis, Henry Slocum, and Joseph Mower.

Union forces destroying Southern rail lines during the March to the Sea. The twisted rails they left behind were dubbed "Sherman's hairpins."

McPherson, and John M. Schofield—against Gen. Joseph E. Johnston's Southerners in early May, driving them all the way to Atlanta by July 8. After sparring with the Confederates for several weeks, Sherman finally forced them to abandon the city on September 2, winning a strategic victory that boosted Northern morale and helped secure Abraham Lincoln's reelection that fall.

On November 15, Sherman began his devastating March to the Sea. Determined to "make Georgia howl," his raiding "bummers" cut a swath 40 miles wide from Atlanta to Savannah, living off the land and destroying the railroads, foodstuffs, and anything else of value to the Southern war effort. His harsh actions, made worse by the unauthorized pillaging undertaken by straggling troopers, were designed solely to force the Confederacy to surrender and not to punish the South, as is commonly thought.

General Sherman arrived in Savannah on December 12, telegraphing President Lincoln that the city was his for Christmas. After wintering there, Sherman's "bummers" began their march northward into the Carolinas on February 1, 1865, capturing Columbia, South Carolina, on the 17th and trapping General Johnston's army near Durham Station, North Carolina, two months later. Sherman offered Johnston extremely generous terms of surrender, which the Southern commander accepted on April 26, effectively ending the war.

William Sherman finished the war second only to Grant as the North's leading war hero. Promoted to lieutenant general on July 25, 1866, he subsequently succeeded Grant as general-in-chief in March 1869 with the rank of full general. General Sherman retired from the Army on November 1, 1883. The following year he was besieged with requests to run for President, which he turned down with his now-famous statement, "I will not accept if nominated and will not serve if elected." William Tecumseh Sherman died in New York City on February 14, 1891, and is buried in St. Louis, Missouri.

Pineville, Louisiana—now Louisiana State University.

After Louisiana seceded from the Union on January 26, 1861, Sherman resigned his position at the military academy and headed North. At the outbreak of the war, he reenlisted in the Army and was commissioned colonel of the 13th U.S. Infantry on May 14. He was assigned command of his brigade shortly thereafter, and he led it with distinction at the First Battle of Bull Run on July 21. Indeed, his was one of the few Union units that didn't break and run at the end of the day. Following this engagement, Sherman was promoted to brigadier general on August 7 and transferred to Kentucky as second-in-command to Gen. Robert Anderson. In Kentucky, he fell victim to unfounded rumors that he was having a nervous breakdown and was reassigned to Cairo, Illinois, in late February 1862. There he joined Gen. Ulysses S. Grant's forces as a division commander.

Sherman first rose to prominence at the Battle of Shiloh in April. Although he was badly surprised by Gen. Albert S. Johnston's attack on the morning of the 6th, he rallied his troops quickly, opposing the Confederate advance on the Union right throughout the day as regiments all round him were driven back. As a result of his determined stand he

became Grant's most trusted commander and was promoted to major general on May 1. Subsequently placed in charge of the 15th Army Corps, General Sherman played a key role in the Vicksburg campaign in spring 1863, spearheading Grant's drive through Mississippi and holding the Union line north of Vicksburg during the ensuing siege.

After the fall of Vicksburg on July 4, Sherman's troops continued to operate in Mississippi until the end of September, when they were directed to aid the beleaguered Union garrison at Chattanooga. Shortly after his arrival, Sherman was promoted to commander of Grant's Army of the Tennessee. On November 25, he led his troops in a bloody assault against Gen. Patrick Cleburne's rebels at the north end of Missionary Ridge during the Battle of Chattanooga. Following this Union victory, the defeated Confederates retreated into Georgia, setting the stage for Sherman's Atlanta Campaign in spring 1864. Succeeding to command of the entire western theater of the war when Grant was named general-in-chief in March, Sherman led his forces—some 100,000 soldiers under Generals George H. Thomas, James B.

The Confederacy

GENERAL
Pierre Gustave Toutant Beauregard   *1818 – 1893*

Commander of the Southern forces that captured Fort Sumter, P.G.T. Beauregard was the first national hero of the Confederacy. A talented but arrogantly proud officer, Beauregard's rise to fame was cut short when he ran afoul of Confederate President Jefferson Davis, and he never achieved the prominence that his early successes promised.

Gustave (as he preferred to be called) was born near New Orleans, Louisiana, on May 28, 1818, the scion of a prominent French Creole family, the Toutant-Beauregards. Following his initial schooling at private academies in New Orleans and New York, Gustave was admitted to West Point, where he graduated second in his class in 1838. He settled in to a career as a professional soldier, serving in Louisiana and as an engineer on Gen. Winfield Scott's staff during the Mexican War.

As the secession crisis was coming to a head late in 1860, Beauregard ironically reached his highest position in the U.S. Army: superintendent of the Military Academy at West Point. By the time he arrived at New York to accept the post, however, Beauregard had made it clear that his loyalties lay with the South, and the War

Department reassigned him after only five days, the shortest tenure of any West Point superintendent. When Louisiana seceded, Gustave resigned his commission in the Army and offered his services to the Confederacy.

Beauregard was commissioned a brigadier general and assigned to oversee the siege of Fort Sumter in Charleston harbor, South Carolina, in March 1861. Under his direction an extensive series of artillery batteries was placed around the harbor, cutting off Sumter from any hope of reinforcement. Finally the fort was pounded into submission on April 12 and 13. The fall of Sumter gave the South its first victory, and Beauregard was instantly transformed into a Confederate hero.

Following his success at Sumter, General Beauregard was named one of the two senior commanders at the First Battle of Bull Run on July 21 (the other was Gen. Joseph E. Johnston). The Confederate victory that day bolstered Beauregard's popularity even further, and he became one of the Confeder-

(opposite) Proud and self-confident, Pierre G.T. Beauregard embodied the spirit of the Confederacy. At the beginning of the war the aristocratic Creole was regarded as a Southern Napoleon.

ate Army's first five lieutenant generals. But the widespread acclaim for the Creole general did not sit well with Jefferson Davis, whom Beauregard had unwisely criticized publicly after Bull Run. Consequently, the Confederate President had him transferred to the western theater of operations early in 1862 to both assist Gen. Albert S. Johnston in his Tennessee campaign and to remove Beauregard from the public spotlight.

On his arrival in the West, Beauregard was ordered by Albert Johnston to reorganize the command. Unfortunately, he used a complex system more suited to the regular Army than the volunteer troops he had to work with, resulting in great confusion at the Battle of Shiloh on April 6. To make matters worse, when Beauregard took over

(right) General Beauregard established his headquarters at Bull Run here in the home of a local farmer Wilmer McLean. Tiring of the fighting near Manassas, McLean subsequently moved to Appomattox Court House, Virginia, where his new home was ironically the site of Lee's surrender to Grant four years later.

(previous pages) Lee and His Generals is a composite wartime print by John Smith. It shows Lee with many of the Southern heroes of the Civil War, including P.G.T. Beauregard, Jeb Stuart, Wade Hampton, Joseph Johnston, Jubal Early, John Breckinridge, Albert Johnston, William Hardee, James Longstreet, Nathan Forrest, John Hood, Stonewall Jackson, John Morgan, Richard Ewell, and Leonidas Polk.

Beauregard prepared the battle plan for the Southern victory at the First Battle of Bull Run, shown here in a Currier and Ives print.

command of the battlefield after Johnston's death, he called off the attack and ordered a retreat back to the Confederate camp at Corinth, Mississippi. The general's actions at Shiloh were widely criticized, and when he subsequently went on sick leave without permission President Davis used his behavior as a convenient excuse to remove him from command in the West.

After recovering his health in August, Gustave was reassigned to the East, first overseeing the coastal defenses of Georgia and South Carolina and later commanding troops near Richmond, Virginia. In spring 1864 he defeated Gen. Benjamin Butler's Union forces at Drewry's Bluff, Virginia, and effectively bottled them up at Bermuda Hundred. His last major service in the war followed in June, when he held off the Federal advance on Petersburg until Robert E. Lee's Army of Northern Virginia could garrison the city, thus beginning the final siege of the war.

After the fall of Atlanta in September 1864, Beauregard was transferred to Georgia, but was unable to stem the Yankees' March

to the Sea with the limited manpower available to him. He finished the war in North Carolina as second-in-command to Gen. Joseph E. Johnston, helping to arrange his old Bull Run comrade's surrender to Gen. William T. Sherman in April 1865.

After the war, Beauregard returned to Louisiana. Turning down offers of high command in the Egyptian and Romanian armies, he spent the rest of his days managing the New Orleans, Jackson & Mississippi Railroad and running the Louisiana state lottery. He died in New Orleans on February 20, 1893.

BRIGADIER GENERAL
John Hunt Morgan *1825 – 1864*

John H. Morgan was, without doubt, one of the Civil War's finest cavalry raiders. Combining the audacity of a Jeb Stuart with the hard-hitting fighting style of Nathan Forrest, Morgan led his forces on raids that reached all the way into the Yankee heartlands of Ohio and Indiana, thereby becoming a legend in his own time.

Morgan was born in Huntsville, Alabama, on June 1, 1825, the son of merchant Calvin Morgan and his wife Henrietta. When John was a boy, his family moved to Lexington, Kentucky, the home of his maternal grandfather and namesake John Wesley Hunt, and it was there that young John received his basic education. After attending Transylvania College for two years, he volunteered for service in the Mexican War and was named a lieutenant in the 1st Kentucky Mounted Volunteers. Returning to Lexington at the end of the war, he invested in hemp and woolen mills and became a successful businessman.

Morgan remained neutral at the beginning of the Civil War but when Kentucky sided with the Union in September 1861, John threw his support to the South. After serving for a few months as captain of the Lexington Rifles, a militia company he had organized in 1857, he was commissioned colonel of the 2nd Kentucky Cavalry (C.S.A.) on April 4, 1862, in recognition of his experience during the Mexican War.

Following service at Shiloh in April, Morgan led his first raid into Kentucky and Tennessee, capturing more than 400 Union soldiers in Columbia on May 1 and destroying the railroad at Cave City on the 11th. On a second foray through central Kentucky in July, he took hundreds more prisoners, capturing extensive supplies as well, and thoroughly disrupting Union operations in that part of the state.

Gen. John H. Morgan, the South's most daring cavalryman.

After taking part in Gen. Braxton Bragg's Kentucky campaign from August through September, 1862, Morgan embarked on yet another independent raid in mid-October. Moving out of Richmond, Kentucky, on the 17th, he captured Lexington and then swung south and west into Tennessee, always striking quickly and withdrawing before pursuing Yankees could catch him. During these operations he heard that a young admirer in Murfreesboro, Tennessee, had told interrogating Federal officers that her name was "Mattie Ready now, but by the grace of God I hope to call myself the wife of John Morgan." Arranging for an introduction, Morgan found her to be a delightful young lady and they

were married on December 14 with Bishop Gen. Leonidas Polk performing the ceremony.

Promoted to brigadier general on December 11, Morgan continued his raids into Union territory through spring 1863, destroying millions of dollars worth of Federal equipment and capturing hundreds of prisoners with minimal losses to his own forces. In recognition of his extraordinary successes, Morgan was voted the thanks of the Confederate Congress for his "varied, heroic, and invaluable services" on May 1.

Shortly thereafter, General Morgan embarked on his most daring raid of all. Taking 2,000 men, he crossed the Ohio River into Indiana on July 8, bringing the war to the North. In 25 days he and his men rode more than 700 miles through Indiana and Ohio, capturing some 5,000 Union soldiers and destroying hundreds of thousands of dollars worth of Yankee railroads and supplies. The

expedition proved too exhausting for Morgan's men and horses, however, and the raider was finally captured by Federal forces at New Lisbon, Ohio, on July 26.

Considered too great a risk for a prisoner of war camp, General Morgan and his command were subsequently jailed in the Ohio State Penitentiary in Columbus. After three months he and six other officers managed to tunnel their way out, escaping on the night of November 27. Three of the escapees were recaptured, but Morgan made his way to the Confederate base at Franklin, Tennessee, by December 23.

After his return, John Morgan was assigned command of all the Confederate cavalry operations in eastern Tennessee and southwestern Virginia. He was killed in a surprise attack at Greenville, Tennessee, on the morning of September 4, 1864. His body was subsequently interred at Lexington, Kentucky.

A Northern view of one of Morgan's raids. Although the Southern general destroyed a good deal of property on his forays, he did not engage in the wanton pillaging shown in this propagandistic print.

GENERAL
Joseph Eggleston Johnston   *1807 – 1891*

Joseph Johnston is probably the most underrated general in the Confederate Army. An experienced and intelligent field commander, his positive achievements have been overshadowed by his inability to perform the series of near-impossible assignments that fell to him in the last years of the war.

Named after his father's Revolutionary War commander, Joseph Johnston was born on February 3, 1807, at Cherry Grove, the family home in Prince Edward County, Virginia. Following studies at the academy in Abingdon, Virginia, Joseph was admitted to West Point in 1825. He graduated 13 out of 46 cadets in 1829 and was commissioned a lieutenant in the artillery.

After serving in the Seminole War, Johnston resigned from the service in 1837 to become a civil engineer, but when he saved a government survey expedition from an Indian attack the following year he was readmitted to the Army as a lieutenant in the elite corps of Topographical Engineers. Joseph became a career officer, serving for 20 years in the engineers, voltigeurs, and cavalry. In 1860, he was appointed quartermaster general of the U.S. Army with the rank of brigadier general.

When Virginia seceded from the Union in April 1861, Johnston resigned from the U.S. Army—the highest ranking officer to do so—and offered his services to his native state. On May 14, he was commissioned a brigadier general in the Confederate Army and assigned command of the troops in the Shenandoah Valley area.

Johnston first displayed his careful but effective style of leadership in the First Bull Run campaign in July 1861. He decoyed a large Federal force into staying at Harpers Ferry while his badly needed troops slipped away to join the Confederate force gathering at Manassas, Virginia. There they proved the deciding factor in the First Battle of Bull

Gen. Joseph Johnston, commander of the Confederate forces in Virginia at the beginning of the war.

Run on the 21st. Johnston, as senior general, assumed command of the Southern force along with P.G.T. Beauregard and decisively directed troop placements on the afternoon of the battle.

Following Bull Run, Joe Johnston was promoted to full general and given command of the Confederate forces in Northern Virginia. During Gen. George B. McClellan's Peninsular campaign in spring 1862, Johnston's troops successfully held the much larger Union forces at Yorktown, Virginia, for a month and then skillfully retreated to Richmond, blocking the Yankees' pursuit at the Battles of Williamsburg and Eltham's

Landing in early May. When McClellan's troops besieged Richmond, he led a daring attack against a portion of the Federal command at Seven Pines on May 31 and June 1. Although the assault failed to rout the Yankees, Johnston succeeded in scaring off McClellan from an attack on Richmond, thereby saving the Confederate capital from imminent capture.

(opposite) Johnston after the war. He died after contracting pneumonia while standing bareheaded at the funeral of his onetime foe, William T. Sherman.

(left) The Battle of Fair Oaks. Johnston was badly wounded in this daring attack against McClellan's forces on the Peninsula, and Robert E. Lee succeeded him as commander of the Confederate forces in northern Virginia.

(below) General Johnston's noble but futile final effort to stop Gen. William T. Sherman's advance at the Battle of Bentonsville, North Carolina, on March 19–21, 1865.

Joe Johnston was badly wounded in the action on the 31st and replaced as commander by Robert E. Lee. When Johnston recovered in November, President Davis reassigned him to command of the Confederate Department of the West, which extended from western Virginia past the Mississippi River into Arkansas and Texas. Johnston did his best to coordinate operations in this vast area, but it proved an impossible task made worse by Jefferson Davis's constant interference. A case in point came during Ulysses S. Grant's Vicksburg campaign, when Johnston ordered the Confederate commander to evacuate the city and save his troops. President Davis countermanded his instructions, resulting in the loss of half of Johnston's army when Vicksburg fell on July 4, 1863.

Johnston was subsequently transferred to northern Georgia in December where he took command of the area's Confederate forces after Gen. Braxton Bragg's defeat at the Battle of Chattanooga. Joe quickly took steps to rebuild Bragg's badly demoralized army, and by spring 1864 he had an effective

The scene of Johnston's surrender to Sherman at Durham Station, North Carolina, on April 26, 1865.

fighting force with which to oppose Gen. William T. Sherman's advance from Chattanooga to Atlanta. Johnston's plan was to lure Sherman's more powerful forces deep into rebel territory, where he could defeat the Yankees on ground of his own choosing. Johnston fought a skillful series of running battles with Sherman's troops during the spring and almost caught the Union general at Kennesaw Mountain on June 17, but in the end the Yankees were too powerful for his limited forces. Retreating to Atlanta, he was removed from command on July 17 by an irate President Davis and replaced by John Hood.

Following the failure of Hood's Tennessee campaign at Nashville, Johnston was reappointed commander of the Confederate forces opposing Sherman on February 23, 1865. Johnston made a gallant last-ditch effort to stop his brilliant opponent at the Battle of Bentonville, in North Carolina, on

March 19–21, but his badly outnumbered troops were no match for Sherman's "bummers." After this defeat Johnston kept his forces in the field until he was given permission to surrender by President Davis on April 18. His capitulation finally came at Durham Station, North Carolina, on April 26, where he received extremely generous terms from Sherman.

After the war, Johnston became an insurance agent in Savannah, Georgia, and Richmond, Virginia. In 1885, he was appointed Federal commissioner of railroads and moved to Washington, D.C. He died there on March 21, 1891, of pneumonia contracted while standing in the rain during the funeral of his onetime and highly respected foe, William T. Sherman.

Phoebe Levy Pember 1823 – 1913

The women of the South, like those in the North, responded to the war by aiding their fighting men in any way they could. Thousands of loyal Confederate ladies organized sewing circles and aid societies to provide clothing, food, and bandages for troops in the field. Many others tended the wounded in hospitals, but none did more than Sally Tompkins and Phoebe Pember.

Phoebe was born into one of the most prominent Jewish families of Charleston, South Carolina, on August 18, 1823. She married Thomas Pember of Boston prior to the war and moved North, but when he contracted tuberculosis they returned South for his health. After Thomas died at Aiken, South Carolina, on July 9, 1861, Phoebe moved back with her parents, then living in Georgia.

Childless and widowed, Mrs. Pember found herself with little to do during the year that followed. When the wife of Confederate Secretary of War George Randolph told her that a woman of her talents was needed at the South's largest military hospital Phoebe Pember immediately volunteered for the job, and in December 1862 she was appointed matron at Chimborazo Hospital in Richmond.

As matron, Mrs. Pember was responsible for overseeing the care of several hundred patients in the hospital's division Number 2. The first female staff member at Chimborazo, Phoebe was not welcomed by the doctors, stewards, and other men she had to work with. She also met resistance from the nurses she supervised, who were recovering soldiers unaccustomed to taking orders from a woman. They did their best to discourage her, but the little widow was strong-willed— she once pulled a pistol on some soldiers who attempted to steal her supply of whis-

Phoebe Pember, dedicated matron of the South's largest hospital.

key—and she soon earned her coworkers's grudging respect. Mrs. Pember had no such problems with her patients, who appreciated her care and dedication. She cooked their meals, dressed their wounds, bathed them, and wrote their letters. Most importantly to the men, she stood up to the doctors for them, questioning orders she felt were improper and demanding better care for her charges.

Mrs. Pember remained at Chimborazo for two-and-a-half years, continuing to care for her patients even after Federal troops had

occupied the city in April 1865. Unafraid of the Yankees, she badgered Federal authorities for hard-to-get supplies, winning their respect and cooperation just as she had the Confederate doctors'.

Phoebe Pember finally left Chimborazo when its last patients were transferred to other hospitals that summer. Returning to her family home in Georgia, she authored a book of reminiscences, *A Southern Woman's Story*, and traveled extensively. Mrs. Pember died in Pittsburgh, Pennsylvania, on March 4, 1913.

A typical wartime general hospital ward. Phoebe Pember saw to the comfort of hundreds of patients in such facilities.

MAJOR GENERAL

George Edward Pickett   *1825 – 1875*

By most accounts George Pickett should not be included in this volume. Although a colorful character, he was a lackluster field commander who accomplished little for the South. But his name is so closely tied to the epic charge at Gettysburg that is viewed as the high-water mark of the Confederacy that he has come to symbolize the Southern soldiers' dedication to duty, earning him a place among the heroes of the Civil War.

George Pickett was born on January 25, 1825, in Richmond, Virginia, the son of Col. Robert Pickett. After attending the Richmond Academy and studying law in his uncle's law office in Quincy, Illinois, George was appointed to the U.S. Military Academy in 1842. He graduated West Point in 1846, dead last in a class that included Thomas Jackson and George McClellan.

Pickett was commissioned a second lieutenant of infantry and sent to the Mexican War, where he gained fame as the first American to enter the fortress of Chapultepec. He remained in the Army after the war, serving in Texas and the Northwest. His most noteworthy service occurred in 1859, when he led a detachment of soldiers onto an island in Puget Sound after an American farmer there was arrested for shooting a Canadian neighbor's hog. The British retaliated by sending three warships in what has become known as the "Pig War" of 1859.

At the outbreak of the Civil War, George resigned his commission in the U.S. Army and made his way cross-country from Washington State to Virginia. Arriving in Richmond in summer 1861, Pickett was commissioned a colonel in the Confederate artillery and assigned to the defenses around Fredericksburg. Promoted to brigadier gen-

Immensely proud and more than a little vain, George Pickett perfumed his flowing curls even while in the field.

eral of infantry on February 13, 1862, he led his troops bravely through the Peninsular campaign later that year, sustaining a severe wound in the Battle of Gaines' Mill on June 27.

General Pickett's wound kept him out of action for several months, causing him to miss the Second Battle of Bull Run and the subsequent Antietam campaign. When he returned to active duty in late September, George was assigned command of a division in Gen. James Longstreet's corps and promoted to major general on October 10. Despite this expanded responsibility, Pickett saw little combat over the following months. At Fredericksburg that December his troops were inactive, and during the Battle of Chancellorsville the following May he was on detached duty with Longstreet in southern Virginia.

George Pickett's first and only major fight as a division commander was the charge at Gettysburg that earned him his place in history. In fact, General Pickett had much less to do with the attack than is popularly believed. His 4,500 soldiers were chosen to spearhead the assault because they were Lee's freshest troops, but they were by no means the only ones involved; the attack included a total of 13,000 Confederates from four different divisions. Pickett organized the attack and gave the order to advance, but while his men were marching the mile toward the Union position on Cemetery Ridge he remained in the rear, leaving it to brigade commanders like Lewis Armistead to lead the ill-fated assault.

Pickett's command was decimated in the charge, suffering about 75 percent casualties. Following Gettysburg they were detailed to North Carolina, where Pickett unsuccessfully attempted to capture New Bern. Returning to Virginia in April 1864, he fought off Gen.

Benjamin Butler's troops at Drewry's Bluff and then rejoined Lee's Army of Northern Virginia at Cold Harbor for the Petersburg campaign. Toward the end of the siege of that city Pickett was assigned to guard the strategically vital crossroads of Five Forks. When Union Gen. Philip H. Sheridan attacked the position on April 1, 1865, Pickett was away at a fish bake, and the rebels lost Five Forks—and with it Petersburg and Richmond. A disgusted Robert E. Lee subsequently removed Pickett from command on April 7, just two days before the surrender at Appomattox Court House.

After the war George Pickett turned down a general's commission in the Egyptian army and became an insurance agent in Norfolk, Virginia. He died there on July 30, 1875, and is buried in Richmond.

John Caball Breckinridge 1821 – 1875

O f all the war's leaders, the onset of the Civil War may have cost John C. Breckinridge the most. A former Vice-President of the United States and a highly respected senator from Kentucky at the onset of hostilities, Breckinridge found himself unjustly branded a traitor by the Union and unwelcome in his home state. Forced into supporting the South, he became one of its most dependable generals and finished his service to the Confederacy as its secretary of war.

Breckinridge was born in Lexington, Kentucky, on January 15, 1821, the son of prominent attorney Joseph Breckinridge. After attending Centre College and the College of New Jersey (now Princeton) John decided to follow in his father's footsteps, studying law in Lexington and at Kentucky's Transylvania College. He opened his practice in Frankfort in 1841, and returned to Lexington in 1845.

After serving briefly in the Mexican War, John Breckinridge turned to politics, winning a seat in the Kentucky legislature in 1849. He was soon elected to the U.S. Congress, where his polished orations and skill at compromise brought him to national attention. As a result, in 1856 he was nominated as James Buchanan's running mate on the Democratic ticket. Winning easily, the 36-year-old Breckinridge was sworn in as the nation's youngest Vice-President on March 4, 1857.

Breckinridge reached the peak of his political career in 1860, when he was nominated for the presidency by the Southern Democrats, who objected to the Northern Democratic candidate, Senator Stephen A. Douglas of Illinois. Although he was defeated by Abraham Lincoln, Breckinridge remained in Washington as the new senator from Kentucky, taking his seat in March 1861 just as the secession crisis was coming to a head. While he himself did not advocate secession,

Breckinridge was a staunch supporter of slavery and actively opposed any efforts to force the Southern states back into the Union at the point of a gun. When the Kentucky legislature voted to support the North in September 1861, his loyalties were questioned because of his antiwar views and a warrant was issued for his arrest. The former Vice-President, then home for a congressional recess, was left with no choice but to cast his lot with the Confederacy, a move that even his enemies later admitted he never wished to make. In December he suffered the added indignity of being formally expelled from the U.S. Senate as a traitor despite the fact that he had resigned two months earlier.

Once he had made his decision to support the South, Breckinridge was welcomed by the Confederate government. Although he had little military experience he was recognized as a natural leader and commissioned a brigadier general on November 2, 1861. The former senator worked out well as a soldier and was promoted to major general in April 1862 after commanding the reserves at the Battle of Shiloh. The following August he distinguished himself by securing the strategically important bluffs overlooking the Mississippi River at Port Hudson, Louisiana,

and in December he led a highly dangerous counterattack at the Battle of Stones River.

After serving in Mississippi and Tennessee in 1863, Breckinridge was transferred to the Shenandoah Valley of Virginia. There, he scored his most decisive victory at the Battle of New Market on May 15, 1864. With a small force that included 247 teenaged cadets from the Virginia Military Institute, Breckinridge was able to rout 6,500 Union soldiers under Gen. Franz Sigel, thereby holding the vitally important Shenandoah Valley for the Confederacy.

After taking part in Gen. Jubal Early's raid on Washington, Breckinridge was appointed Confederate secretary of war on February 5, 1865. Unable to stem the South's inevitable defeat at that late date, he did his best to ease the last days of the Confederacy. After coordinating the evacuation of the government from Richmond in April, he headed to North Carolina with the rest of President Davis's cabinet. There, in his final service to the Confederacy, he assisted in negotiating Gen. Joseph E. Johnston's treaty of surrender with Gen. William T. Sherman.

After the surrender, Breckinridge made his way to Florida, sailing from there to Cuba and then Europe. He returned to his beloved Kentucky in 1869, resuming the practice of law, but thereafter refused any involvement in politics. He died in Lexington on May 17, 1875.

(opposite) John C. Breckinridge at the pinnacle of his political career as Vice-President of the United States.

(left) The Virginia Military Academy cadets at the Battle of New Market. **Breckinridge, concerned with the boys' safety, refused to put them into combat until all of his other reserves were exhausted, but once engaged they proved the deciding factor in the battle.**

LIEUTENANT GENERAL
Ambrose Powell Hill *1825 – 1865*

Robert E. Lee's daring operations in the field were not without their dangers. On more than one occasion, it was Ambrose P. Hill and his famed Light Division that made the difference between brilliant victory and defeat for Lee's Army of Northern Virginia.

A. P. Hill was born at Culpeper, Virginia, on November 9, 1825, the son of Major Thomas Hill. After attending Simms Academy, he was appointed to West Point in 1842, where he roomed with George McClellan. Although he didn't graduate until 1847 because of deficiencies in chemistry and philosophy, he still managed to finish in the middle of his class of 38 cadets. Brief service in the Mexican War followed, as did postings in Florida and Texas. Then he was transferred to Washington, D.C., in 1855, where he married Kitty Morgan, the sister of John Hunt Morgan.

Hill resigned his commission from the U.S. Army on March 1, 1861, and was subsequently appointed colonel of the 13th Virginia Infantry. Following campaigns in western and northern Virginia, he was promoted to brigadier general on February 26, 1862.

General Hill first displayed the fighting style that would make him famous during the Peninsular campaign in spring 1862. Fending off the Federal pursuit of Gen. Joseph E. Johnston's retreating troops at the Battle of Williamsburg on May 5, Hill's brigade suffered heavy casualties but held the line. He was promoted to major general on May 26. The brigade also played a leading role in the Seven Days' Battles in June. Growing tired of waiting for Stonewall Jackson's exhausted troops to open the fighting at Beaver Dam Creek on June 26, Hill started the battle himself, stunning McClellan's Yankees and forcing them south. He continued to pound the Federals at Gaines' Mill and White Oak Swamp, solidifying his reputation as a tough fighter and earning his fast-moving troops their nickname, the "Light Division."

Ambrose P. Hill, commander of the Army of Northern Virginia's famed Light Division.

Assigned to Stonewall Jackson's command after the Seven Days' Battles, Ambrose quickly proved his worth by saving his commander's assault at Cedar Mountain on August 9. Indeed, Jackson was being pushed back by a heavy Federal counterattack when the Light Division crashed into the Yankees' right flank and drove Union Gen. Nathaniel P. Banks from the field. At the Second Battle of Bull Run on August 29 and 30, Hill anchored the left of Jackson's line, holding the position in the face of repeated Union assaults.

Hill's greatest service to the South occurred during Lee's Antietam campaign that September. After helping Jackson to capture the Federal garrison at Harpers Ferry on the 15th, Hill's command remained behind to take care of prisoners while the rest of Stonewall's troops joined Lee outside Sharpsburg, Maryland. When the Battle of Antietam began outside Sharpsburg on the morning of the 17th, Hill marched his Light Division the 18 miles from Harpers Ferry at the double-quick. They arrived on the field just as the Union Army was beginning to mount a heavy assault against the south end of Lee's line.

(above) Hill's division entering Gettysburg. His infantrymen began the battle northwest of the village on the morning of July 1, 1863. Here they are seen charging across McPherson's Ridge toward the Union troops on Seminary Ridge (center).

(right) Burnside Bridge, at the southern end of the Antietam battlefield. Hill's division was instrumental in driving back Union Gen. Ambrose Burnside's assault in this sector of the battle.

Undaunted, Hill's troops drove the Yankees from the battlefield, saving Lee from almost certain defeat.

At the Battle of Fredericksburg that December, Hill commanded the section of the rebel line that was breached by Gen. George G. Meade's assault. Holding their ground until reinforcements arrived, Hill's troops — particularly those under the command of James Archer — once again helped save the Army of Northern Virginia from possible disaster.

The Battle of Cedar Mountain, Virginia. Here Hill's troops routed the Union forces under Gen. Nathaniel Banks.

Hill succeeded to the command of Jackson's corps when Stonewall was mortally wounded after his daring flank attack at Chancellorsville on May 2, 1863. In the reorganization of the Army of Northern Virginia that followed Jackson's death, Hill was promoted to lieutenant general and given command of Lee's 3rd Corps, which he led for the remainder of the war. The corps opened the Battle of Gettysburg for the South on July 1, receiving heavy casualties in McPherson's Woods but finally driving off the Yankees on their front. General Hill, who was unwell, remained in the rear and took little part in the battle, however.

Hill's physical condition was to affect him for the rest of the war. Following the Battle of the Wilderness in May 1864, he was so incapacitated that he had to go on leave, missing the Battle of Spotsylvania. After enduring months on the siege lines of Petersburg, he was again forced to take leave in March 1865. Recuperating at his home in the city, Hill rushed back to his troops when he heard the noise of the final Federal assault on April 2 and was killed trying to rally his command. He is buried in Richmond beneath a monument raised by his former soldiers.

Stand Watie   1806 – 1871

Stand Watie is one of the Confederacy's least-known commanders and its most unusual general. A three-quarter Cherokee, he led a band of Confederate Indians in an effective campaign of guerrilla warfare throughout the war.

Stand Watie, or De-gata-ga, was born near Rome, Georgia, on December 12, 1806, the son of a full-blood Cherokee father and a half-blood mother. After attending a missionary school in Cornwall, Connecticut, he returned to Georgia, where he edited an Indian newspaper with his brother Elias and became a leader of the Cherokee people.

In 1835 Watie was one of four tribal officials who signed a treaty whereby the Cherokees agreed to sell their extensive lands in Georgia and promised to move to the Indian Territory, now Oklahoma. The measure badly divided the tribe—Watie was the only signer who escaped assassination—and had major repercussions 30 years later during the Civil War.

Stand Watie moved to Oklahoma with the rest of the Cherokees in 1839 and became a successful planter. When the War Between the States broke out in 1861, he and his followers sided with the Confederacy while those opposed to the 1835 treaty supported the North, blaming Southern landowners for forcing them from Georgia. After organizing a company of Indian soldiers, he was commissioned a colonel in the Confederate Army on July 12, 1861, and authorized to raise a regiment of mounted rifles among the Cherokee, Creek, Seminole, and Osage tribes. He formally entered the war at the Battle of Wilson's Creek, Missouri, on August 10, helping to win that early Confederate victory. At the Battle of Pea Ridge, Arkansas, the following March, he and his Indians anchored the Confederate right, holding the rebel line until it was overwhelmed by Union forces on the battle's second day.

Watie's troops were outfitted much like these Indian soldiers in the Federal Army.

Following Pea Ridge, Colonel Watie's Mounted Rifles undertook a campaign of guerrilla warfare in Arkansas and the Indian Territory. Their daring hit-and-run raids against the Federal troops and Northern Cherokees were highly effective, and Watie's Indians soon became the Confederacy's most

Stand Watie, the Confederacy's Cherokee General. He was the South's most effective leader in the far West.

important strike force in the area. In recognition of this, the Cherokee colonel was promoted to brigadier general on May 6, 1864.

General Watie's greatest triumph occurred on June 15, 1864, when he and his troopers attacked a Union supply boat, the *J. R. Williams*, as it steamed up the Arkansas River and, with artillery and rifle fire, drove it aground. After they removed food and uniforms and other stores valued at more than $100,000, they fired the ship and sent it floating back down the river in a final gesture of defiance to the Yankees.

General Watie continued fighting in the Indian Territory until June 1865, a full month after the Confederate forces in the Far West formally surrendered. Watie finally laid down his arms at Doaksville on June 23, the last Confederate general to surrender. Afterward, he returned to his property at Honey Creek, Oklahoma, to raise tobacco. Stand Watie died there on September 9, 1871.

LIEUTENANT GENERAL
James Longstreet   1821 – 1904

James Longstreet was second only to Stonewall Jackson among Robert E. Lee's commanders in the Army of Northern Virginia. Lee called the general his "Old War Horse," for he served the South faithfully from First Bull Run to Appomattox Court House; and despite an error in judgment at Gettysburg that cast a shadow over him for the rest of his life, Longstreet remained one of the giants of the Confederate Army.

James Longstreet was born on January 8, 1821, in Edgefield District, South Carolina. Moving to Georgia while a young child, James was raised near Augusta and in Somerville, Alabama, where his family moved after his father's death in 1833. Admitted to West Point from Alabama in 1838, James graduated near the bottom of his class in 1842.

Lieutenant Longstreet's first assignment after leaving the military academy was with the 4th U.S. Infantry at Jefferson Barracks, Missouri. While stationed there the young officer became friends with another recent West Point grad who would have a profound effect on Longstreet's life, even marrying his cousin Julia Dent. The former cadet's name was Ulysses S. Grant.

Following subsequent infantry duty in Louisiana, in Florida, and in the Mexican War, Longstreet was transferred to the paymaster's department. He was serving in Albuquerque, New Mexico Territory, when the Civil War broke out. After slowly making

his way east, Longstreet resigned from the U.S. Army on June 1 and offered his services to the Confederacy, fully expecting to be named paymaster. He was given a field command instead, and commissioned a brigadier general on June 17.

General Longstreet began his service to the South in an auspicious way, successfully defending the Confederate line against the first Federal assault in the first major battle of the war. While positioned at Blackburn's Ford on Bull Run Creek on July 18, 1861, Longstreet's well-placed troops turned back a heavy Yankee reconnaissance probe, giving the Southern forces at Manassas an important boost in morale before the First Battle of Bull Run on the 21st. Longstreet was promoted to major general on October 17.

Longstreet solidified his reputation as a fighting man during the Peninsular campaign, in spring 1862. Although confusing orders caused him to fail in his assigned role in the Battle of Seven Pines on June 1, he more than redeemed himself during the Seven Days' Battles that were fought after Robert E. Lee assumed command of the

(opposite) A tough fighter, "Old Pete" Longstreet was one of Robert E. Lee's finest infantry commanders.

Confederate forces on the Peninsula. His hard-hitting assaults against Gen. George B. McClellan's Union troops quickly brought Longstreet to Lee's attention, and he was subsequently assigned command of over half of the Army of Northern Virginia's infantry.

Longstreet confirmed his value to Lee at the Second Battle of Bull Run by routing the attacking Union troops on the morning of August 30 and winning the battle for the South. After holding the Confederate line at the Battles of South Mountain and Antietam in September, Longstreet—by then known affectionately as "Old Pete" among his men—was promoted to Lee's senior lieutenant general on October 9. At the Battle of Fredericksburg on December 13, Longstreet commanded the northern end of Lee's line, overseeing the sanguinary defense of Marye's Heights by Gen. Lafayette McLaws's troops.

Old Pete was detailed to southern Virginia on forage duty in spring 1863, missing the

Plum Run Valley, Gettysburg. General Longstreet's forces fought their way across this rock-strewn lowland while trying to capture Little Round Top on the second day of the battle. The heavy casualties here caused the area to be dubbed the "Slaughter Pen."

120

Battle of Chancellorsville, but he returned north in time to take part in what would become his most controversial fight—the Battle of Gettysburg. The Old War Horse disagreed with Lee's plan to have him attack the southern end of the Union line on July 2, during the second day of fighting, and petulantly delayed his assault until late in the afternoon, giving Federal Gen. Daniel Sickles time to block his advance. Longstreet thus lost the South's best opportunity to drive the Yankees from Cemetery Ridge and win the battle—and possibly the war. The mistake would haunt him for the rest of his life.

The fall of Richmond, April 2, 1865. **After Grant's troops broke through Lee's lines at Petersburg, Longstreet was forced to abandon the Confederate capital and join in Lee's retreat toward Appomattox.**

After Gettysburg, Longstreet was transferred to Tennessee to assist Gen. Braxton Bragg. There, at the Battle of Chickamauga on September 20, Old Pete scored one of his most decisive victories, smashing through the Union line and scattering most of Gen. William Rosecrans's Yankees.

Lee's "Old War Horse" returned to Virginia in May 1864, just in time (literally) to save the rest of the Army of Northern Virginia at the Battle of the Wilderness. Longstreet's troops completed their march to the battlefield early on May 6 as a Union assault was breaking through the southern end of Lee's defenses. Without pausing, Old Pete's rebels mounted a counterattack against the Yankees, rolling up their flank and saving Lee from likely defeat. Unfortunately, Longstreet was badly wounded during the attack (accidently hit by one of his own men just

miles from where Stonewall Jackson was similarly wounded a year earlier) and forced to relinquish command. After his recovery Old Pete was assigned to the defenses of Richmond. When the Confederate forces evacuated the city on April 2, 1865, Longstreet joined General Lee on the Army of Northern Virginia's final march, staying with him until the surrender at Appomattox Court House a week later.

After the war, Longstreet lived in New Orleans and in Gainesville, Georgia. Joining the Republican party during Reconstruction—which made him very unpopular in the South—he succeeded in getting several government appointments through the influence of his old friend Ulysses S. Grant. After serving as U.S. minister to Turkey and as a U.S. marshal in Georgia, James Longstreet died in Gainesville on January 2, 1904.

(right) Henry House Hill in the Manassas National Military Park. At the climax of the Second Battle of Bull Run in August 1862, Longstreet's troops routed John Pope's Yankees across these fields.

(below) Exhausted and half-starved, their cause lost, Longstreet's soldiers furl their battle flag one last time before their surrender at Appomattox Court House.

John Pelham *1838 – 1863*

Heroic leadership was not just limited to generals during the War Between the States. One of the bravest, most effective officers in the Confederacy was the man called the South's "boy major"—23-year-old John Pelham.

Born in Benton (now Calhoun) County, Alabama, on September 14, 1838, Pelham was the son of prominent planter and physician Dr. Atkinson Pelham. John was admitted to a special five-year course of study at West Point in 1856, and became an expert in artillery tactics. With the coming of the Civil War he resigned from the Military Academy just weeks before his graduation, on April 22, 1861, to join the Confederate Army.

Pelham was commissioned a lieutenant and assigned to the Wise Virginia Artillery. After distinguishing himself on Henry House Hill at the First Battle of Bull Run in July 1861, he was promoted to captain and given command of the highly mobile horse artillery attached to Jeb Stuart's cavalry. Pelham's unit first proved itself a force to be reckoned with during the Peninsular campaign in 1862. After it served with distinction at Yorktown, Williamsburg, and the Seven Days' Battles Jeb Stuart had John promoted to major on August 16 with the comment that "no field grade is too high for his merit and capacity." The boy major soon confirmed Stuart's confidence. At Second Bull Run two weeks later he saved Stonewall Jackson's troops from a Union flank attack, and at Antietam in September he moved his artillery with such speed and accuracy that the Yankees were convinced that he commanded two batteries instead of just one.

John Pelham's finest service to the Confederacy occurred at the Battle of Fredericksburg. Opposing the Union assault south of

The Confederacy's "boy major," artilleryman John Pelham.

the city on the morning of December 13, Pelham advanced his battery to an open position between the lines so he could get a clearer zone of fire. Although his guns were badly mauled by Federal artillery John kept firing until he ran out of ammunition, holding back the Yankee attack for two hours. Watching "the gallant Pelham" as he took the place of a wounded crewman during the cannonade, an impressed Robert E. Lee declared, "It is glorious to see such courage in one so young!"

Pelham's courage was to be his undoing. On March 17, 1863, while in camp with Stuart's cavalry near Kelly's Ford, Virginia, the boy major heard that a fight was shaping up with some Yankee horsemen. Never having been in a cavalry charge, he joined in just for the excitement. During the fight, John Pelham was severely wounded by an exploding artillery shell, and he died later that day at the home of his fiancée in nearby Culpeper.

The passing of the gallant Pelham was mourned throughout the South; several women are said to have donned widow's weeds in his memory. His friend and commander Jeb Stuart was particularly grieved. He arranged for Pelham's body to be laid in state in the Confederate capital, and even named his daughter Virginia Pelham Stuart in honor of the boy major. John Pelham was subsequently immortalized as a popular hero in John Esten Cooke's 1894 novel *Surry of Eagle's Nest*.

(top) Fredericksburg, Virginia, from the South. **During the battle in 1862, Pelham's troops occupied part of Stonewall Jackson's line on the high ground to the left.**

(above) Federal artillery opposite Fredericksburg. **During the battle on December 13, 1862, Pelham duelled with these guns, which were commanded by his former West Point artillery instructor, Gen. Henry Hunt.**

Raphael Semmes 1809 – 1877

For the Confederacy, the War Between the States was primarily fought on land. The South had few warships, and had neither the time nor the money to develop a large Navy. But what the Confederate naval forces lacked in size, they made up for in the talents of their leading naval officer, the legendary commander of C.S.S. *Alabama*, Raphael Semmes.

Semmes was born in Charles County, Maryland, on September 17, 1809, but was raised in the Georgetown district of Washington, D.C., by his uncle and namesake after both of his parents died.

Young Raphael was appointed a midshipman in the U.S. Navy on April 1, 1826. After study at the Naval School in Norfolk, Virginia, and extensive service on the southern coast of the United States, he was commissioned a lieutenant on February 9, 1837. During these years, frequent shore duty enabled him to study law, and he was admitted to the bar in 1834.

At the outbreak of the Mexican War, Semmes was given command of the brig *Somers*, and he earned a commendation for saving much of his crew when the ship unexpectedly sank in a storm in December 1846. Following this loss, he served with the naval forces assigned to shore duty in Mexico, participating in the campaigns against Vera Cruz and Mexico City and earning several citations for bravery. At the close of the war, Semmes returned to duty on the Gulf coast, settling in Mobile, Alabama.

(right) Raphael Semmes, the South's most daring Naval commander. **His men called him "Old Beeswax" because of his heavily waxed moustache.**

(opposite) The battle between C.S.S. **Alabama** *and U.S.S.* **Kearsarge.** **Trapped in the harbor of Cherbourg, France, Semmes opted to fight the larger Federal gunboat rather than abandon his ship. The celebrated French artist Édouard Manet painted this picture after witnessing the battle.**

Semmes resigned from the U.S. Navy on February 15, 1861, as the secession crisis came to a head. Enlisting in the Confederate Navy, he was commissioned a commander and sent North to purchase munitions. Indeed, he succeeded in getting large quantities shipped South before war was declared. (Gallantly, he never revealed the names of the Northern merchants who thus fueled the Confederacy's war effort.)

When war broke out in April, Semmes was assigned to disrupt the Northern economy by attacking merchant vessels on the high seas. After converting the packet boat *Havana* into the warship *Sumter* he steamed out of New Orleans on June 30 and quickly captured 12 U.S. vessels in the Caribbean. Turning his course toward Europe, he captured another six American merchantmen on their way across the Atlantic, no mean feat at a time when neither radar nor radio existed to help one locate ships on the high seas. In recognition of his success, Commander Semmes was promoted to captain and voted the thanks of the Confederate Congress.

On his arrival off the European coast in April 1862, Semmes put into port at Gibraltar for repairs. There *Sumter* was quickly trapped by a blockade of Union warships and he was forced to sell the boat and discharge his crew in port. Captain Semmes did not remain idle for long, however. While making his way back to the Confederacy he was ordered to take command of a new ship that had just been completed for him: C.S.S. *Alabama*.

Semmes began his new command off the Azores on August 24. Moving into the mid-Atlantic, he captured ten whalers and then headed toward the American coast, where he bagged a total of 45 ships over the next several months, including the U.S. Navy gunboat *Hatteras*. Setting his course eastward in July 1863 he steamed around the African coast and into the Indian Ocean, making it all the way to Singapore before turning back in December. Arriving off the European coast in June 1864, after capturing nine more U.S. ships, Captain Semmes steamed *Alabama* into Cherbourg, France, for repairs. Trapped in the harbor by the U.S. Navy cruiser *Kearsarge*, he tried to fight his way out. On June 19, 1864, in one of the most famous naval duels in history, *Kearsarge* sank *Alabama* in

little over an hour, ending the story of the finest raider of the Confederacy.

Captain Semmes went down with his ship—but was rescued by a British yacht and thus avoided capture by the Yankees on *Kearsarge*. He returned to the Confederacy in January 1865, was promoted to rear admiral and was assigned command of the Confederate naval forces protecting Richmond. When the Confederate capital fell on April 2, Semmes scuttled his ships and organized his sailors as a brigade of footsoldiers. Immediately commissioned a brigadier general by Jefferson Davis, Semmes led his troops into North Carolina, where he surrendered as part of Gen. Joseph E. Johnston's command on April 26. Semmes was subsequently arrested on charges of piracy but was released after four months without trial.

After the war Semmes tried his hand at several occupations, including college professor and editor of the *Memphis Daily Bulletin*, but was driven from them by the political pressures of Reconstruction. He finally settled into a legal career in Alabama until his death in Mobile on August 30, 1877.

MAJOR GENERAL
Patrick Ronayne Cleburne *1828 – 1864*

Unlike the Union, which had numerous generals from Germany, Ireland, and other countries, the South had few foreign-born officers. Patrick Cleburne was one of only two immigrants who became major generals in the Confederate Army. He was also one of the South's best field commanders. Known as the "Stonewall Jackson of the West," Cleburne fought bravely at battles from Shiloh to Franklin.

Patrick Cleburne was born in County Cork, Ireland, on St. Patrick's Day, March 17, 1828. Trained as a pharmacist—his father was a physician—he was greatly embarrassed at failing his licensing exam in 1846 and enlisted in the British infantry, where he received his military training. Emigrating to America in 1849, Cleburne settled in Helena, Arkansas, working in a drug store and studying law. He was admitted to the bar in 1856 and soon developed a thriving practice.

Pat Cleburne performed his first military service for the South before Arkansas had even seceded. In February 1861, the Yell Rifles, a volunteer infantry unit to which Cleburne belonged, helped seize the Federal arsenal at Little Rock. When Arkansas joined the Confederacy in May, the Yell Rifles enlisted in what would become the 15th Arkansas Infantry, with Pat as their captain. The intelligent, experienced officer quickly advanced to colonel of the 15th, and by early 1862 was a brigadier general serving in Gen. William Hardee's command. Cleburne made his mark as a tough, aggressive field commander at the Battle of Shiloh in April. Leading a brigade on the Confederate left during the first day's fight, he practically drove the Yankees on his front into the Tennessee River. After the Union counterattack the following morning, his brigade acted

Patrick Cleburne, one of the Confederacy's finest commanders in the west.

The Battle of Perryville, Kentucky, where Cleburne held the Confederate left against repeated Union attacks.

as rear guard for the retreating rebel army. Following this, at the Battle of Richmond in Kentucky on August 30, Cleburne's troops captured more than 4,000 Federal prisoners. Although Pat was badly wounded by a bullet in his mouth, he was well enough by October to lead his troops again at the Battle of Perryville in Kentucky.

Commissioned a major general on December 13, 1862, Cleburne soon proved that he was deserving of the promotion at the Battle of Stones River. His division crumpled the south end of the Union line on the morn-

ing of December 31, driving the Yankees almost a mile and a half northward. His attack was stopped only when an equally hard-fighting Union general, Philip Sheridan, organized a defensive line to the rear.

After Stones River, Cleburne saw little combat until the Battle of Chickamauga on September 19 and 20, 1863. There, his troops made repeated assaults against Gen. George H. Thomas's position, but even Cleburne was unable to break through the "Rock of Chickamauga."

Cleburne's finest hour occurred during the Battle of Chattanooga, which followed in November. He held the north end of Missionary Ridge against multiple attacks by Gen. William T. Sherman's troops on the 25th, abandoning the position only after the rest of the Confederate line had been routed. The next day Cleburne's men fought a desperate rear-guard action at Ringgold Gap, Georgia, saving the South's artillery from capture and earning their commander a vote of thanks by the Confederate Congress.

In the winter following Chattanooga, Cleburne drafted a controversial plan for easing the Southern army's manpower shortage, which was becoming critical. His sug-gestion to allow slaves to fight, granting them their freedom if they did, was quickly dismissed, however, and probably cost the well-intentioned general promotion to the higher command he deserved.

Cleburne remained with his division through the Atlanta campaign of 1864. After the fall of that city he was killed in action at the Battle of Franklin, in Tennessee, on November 30, 1864, while bravely leading a charge on foot after two horses had been shot out from under him. Patrick Cleburne's death was mourned throughout the South.

The Confederate retreat from Chattanooga. **Cleburne earned a vote of thanks from Congress for his rear-guard defense against the pursuing forces of William T. Sherman following the Battle of Missionary Ridge on November 25, 1863.**

James Ewell Brown Stuart   1833 – 1864

★ ★ ★ ★ ★ ★ ★ ★ ★ ★ ★ ★ ★ ★ ★ ★

No one embodied the Confederate ideal of chivalry more than the Army of Northern Virginia's colorful cavalry commander, James Ewell Brown ("Jeb") Stuart. A bold and daring raider who always remained a gentleman, Stuart reveled in the role of a 19th-century knight errant and was idolized throughout the South.

Jeb Stuart was born on February 6, 1833, at Laurel Hill, his family home in Patrick County, Virginia. After receiving his basic schooling at Wytheville, Virginia, he attended Emory and Henry College for two years. He then entered the U.S. Military Academy in 1850. Jeb—nicknamed "Beauty" for his good looks—graduated West Point 13 out of 46 cadets in 1854 and was appointed to the mounted rifles. After several months in Texas, Lieutenant Stuart was transferred to the newly established 1st U.S. Cavalry in Kansas, where he served under Col. Joseph E. Johnston. While in Kansas, he married Flora Cooke, daughter of Col. Philip St. George Cooke, commander of the dragoons at Fort Leavenworth.

In 1859 Stuart traveled to Washington, D.C., to promote his design of a new clasp for carrying cavalry sabers. There he was dispatched to Arlington, Virginia, with orders directing Col. Robert E. Lee to quell John Brown's insurrection at Harpers Ferry. Jeb, who had known Lee from his days at West Point, accompanied the colonel as his aide and took a leading role in the capture of Brown on October 18.

Jeb Stuart returned to Kansas after the raid on Harpers Ferry, remaining there until early 1861. With the onset of the secession crisis, he secured leave from his post and headed east to offer his services to the South. He resigned from the U.S. Army on May 14 and was commissioned a captain in the Confederate cavalry ten days later. Subsequently appointed colonel of the 1st Virginia Cavalry in July, Stuart successfully screened Gen. Joseph E. Johnston's withdrawal from the

(above) Stuart first rose to fame by riding completely around General McClellan's army on the Virginia Peninsula in 1862.

(opposite) With his flowing beard and ornate uniform, Jeb Stuart revelled in his role as a Southern cavalier.

Federal cavalrymen pursuing Stuart's troopers on the Peninsula. **Stuart's ride was enormously embarrassing to McClellan's cavalry commander —Stuart's father-in-law, Gen. Philip Cooke.**

Shenandoah Valley before the First Battle of Bull Run. After leading a decisive charge at that battle, Jeb was promoted to brigadier general on September 21 and given command of all of Johnston's cavalry.

General Stuart first displayed the daring style that became his trademark during the Peninsular campaign in the spring of 1862. Asked by General Lee to gather information on the deployments of George McClellan's Army of the Potomac, Jeb led his command of 1,200 troopers completely around the Union Army between June 12 and 15, capturing hundreds of prisoners and horses in

the process and, in turn, losing only one man. The 100-mile raid earned Stuart his reputation as a bold adventurer and was extremely embarrassing to McClellan's Yankees—particularly to his chief of cavalry, Jeb's father-in-law Philip Cooke. As a result of this bold maneuver, Jeb was promoted to major general on July 25 and given command of all of the Army of Northern Virginia's cavalry.

After distinguished service at the Second Battle of Bull Run and the Antietam campaign that summer, Stuart set out on a raid northward to cut General McClellan's supply lines in October. Crossing the Potomac River near Harpers Ferry on the 10th, Stuart's

troopers rode as far as Chambersburg, Pennsylvania, capturing extensive stores but failing to destroy the strategic railroad bridge there (which was made of iron and couldn't be burned). The following day they swung to the southeast, baffling the pursuing Yankee cavalry and riding completely around McClellan's army once again before they returned to Virginia late on the 11th.

In the months that followed, Stuart continued to build his reputation as one of the South's leading officers. At Fredericksburg in December, his field artillery under Maj. John Pelham played an important role in the battle, and at Chancellorsville in May 1863 he briefly succeeded to the command of Stonewall Jackson's corps after both Jackson and A.P. Hill were wounded. During the

The Rebels under Stuart leaving Chambersburg —

Gettysburg campaign in June and July, however, Jeb's overweening fondness for spectacular raids led to one incident that has tarnished his record as a soldier. Widely expanding upon General Lee's discretionary orders, Stuart led his command on yet another ride around the Federal Army and, as a result, deprived Lee of vital intelligence and most of his cavalry cover during his march into Pennsylvania. By the time Stuart arrived at Gettysburg on July 2, it was too late for him to take a major role in the battle. He led a cavalry assault east of town on the 3rd, but was quickly repulsed by Federal horsemen under Judson Kilpatrick and George A. Custer.

Jeb Stuart continued to lead Lee's cavalry through the Battle of the Wilderness on May 5–6, 1864. At the conclusion of the battle, as Lee started marching south to Spotsylvania Court House, Union cavalry commander

(above) The Cavalry of the Army of Northern Virginia in Chambersburg, Pennsylvania, on October 10, 1862. Stuart's forces captured many badly needed horses and other supplies in this raid.

Philip H. Sheridan led a force of 12,000 toward Richmond hoping to cut off Lee from the Confederate capital. Stuart's 4,500 troopers intercepted Sheridan's Yankees at Yellow Tavern, Virginia, on May 11, and in the ensuing fight General Stuart was mortally wounded. Carried to Richmond, Jeb Stuart died on May 12, 1864, and is buried in the city's Hollywood Cemetery.

A monument in Richmond, Virginia, commemorates the Confederacy's beloved Cavalry officer.

Belle Boyd   1843 – 1900

At the outset of the War Between the States neither the North nor the South had a formal military intelligence system. Both sides got their information from an assortment of paid agents and volunteer spies, some of them reliable, many not. One of the best of the Confederacy's civilian spies was Belle Boyd. Despite her youth she proved to be a daring and resourceful operative, providing Stonewall Jackson with invaluable intelligence about Yankee troop movements around the Shenandoah Valley.

Belle was born in Martinsburg, in what is now West Virginia, on May 9, 1843, the daughter of storekeeper Benjamin Boyd. When Virginia seceded in 1861, Benjamin enlisted in the 2nd Virginia Infantry, leaving Belle and the rest of his family to fend for themselves in Martinsburg. Belle proved up to the task when a Yankee soldier pushed his way into the Boyd residence on the Fourth of July insisting that the household fly the Stars and Stripes. Belle ordered him to leave and, when he refused, pulled out a pistol and shot him. Pleading self-defense, she went unpunished by Union authorities.

Belle quickly realized that accurate information on Federal troop movements could prove valuable to her father's unit, which was part of Stonewall Jackson's brigade, and she began bringing reports to Jackson's headquarters. Belle proved an excellent agent. Self-possessed and intelligent—she was a graduate of Mount Washington College—Belle was only a girl of 18 and could move around the countryside without arousing suspicion. Even when Union soldiers first caught her with incriminating notes in her possession, she was dismissed as a silly schoolgirl and let go with a warning.

By early 1862 the Federal authorities began taking Belle more seriously, and she was arrested and jailed in Baltimore. On her return to Martinsburg in the spring she was kept under such close scrutiny that spying

Although no beauty, Belle Boyd's sparkling personality enabled her to charm secrets from dozens of Union Army officers.

there was impossible, so she went to visit her aunt in Front Royal, at the northern end of Virginia's Shenandoah Valley. Upon her arrival, she found that her aunt's house had been commandeered by Union Gen. James Shields, who was fighting Stonewall Jackson's forces in the Valley. Belle made the most of the situation, playing up to Shields's aide to get information and even eavesdropping on one of the general's war councils. She rode 15 miles to Jackson's camp that night to deliver some vital information that she'd overheard, and returned to Front Royal before she was missed the next morning.

Belle's most important service to the Confederacy occurred during the Battle of Front Royal on May 23, 1862. As Jackson's troops advanced on the town, she saw that the Yankees were beginning to retreat and might

escape if the Confederates didn't move quickly. Riding between the enemy lines as the fighting went on around her, Belle managed to deliver this message to General Jackson, enabling him to capture more than 600 prisoners.

After Union forces retook Front Royal in July, Belle was twice arrested and confined in Washington prisons. When she was finally released, she made her way south to Richmond. In 1864 she sailed for Europe on a Southern blockade runner, but the ship was captured at sea by a U.S. Navy vessel. Belle, again making the most of her situation, worked her considerable charms on the young Naval lieutenant who captured her, and by the time they returned to his home base in the U.S. they were engaged to be married! They wed—after he was discharged from the service—and eventually moved to England. After the war Belle took up acting and returned to America around 1867. She died of a heart attack on June 11, 1900, while on tour in Kilbourne, Wisconsin.

LIEUTENANT GENERAL
Joseph Wheeler   *1836 – 1906*

While Joseph Wheeler is best known as the valued Confederate general who commanded the Southern cavalry in the West during the War Between the States, he also distinguished himself as a major general in the U.S. Army during the Spanish-American War, achieving the highest rank of any former officer of the Confederacy.

Wheeler was born near Augusta, Georgia, on September 10, 1836. After a limited education, he was appointed to the U.S. Military Academy in 1854, graduating 19 out of 22 cadets in 1859. Appointed a lieutenant of mounted rifles, he was assigned to duty fighting Indians in the Far West.

With the onset of the Civil War, Wheeler resigned his commission in the U.S. Army on April 22, 1861. Enlisting in the Confederate Army, he was commissioned a lieutenant of artillery but was promoted, on September 4, to colonel of the 19th Alabama Infantry. After leading this unit at the Battle of Shiloh in April 1862, he was reassigned to the cavalry and remained with that branch of the service for the rest of the war.

Given command of Braxton Bragg's cavalry brigade on September 14, 1862, Wheeler soon demonstrated the aggressive style that earned him the nickname "Fighting Joe." During Bragg's Kentucky campaign that fall, he anchored the Confederate right at the Battle of Perryville on October 8 and effectively screened Bragg's return to Tennessee at the end of the month. In recognition of his service, Fighting Joe was promoted to brigadier general on October 30. Just three months later, following meritorious action at the Battle of Stones River on December 31, he was named a major general.

As the war drew on, Wheeler continued to build his reputation as one of the South's best cavalry commanders. Following the Battle of Chickamauga in September 1863,

Gen. Joseph Wheeler in his 20s, while serving as one of the South's finest cavalry commanders.

he led the Confederate attack against the supply line of the retreating Yankees. He destroyed miles of strategic railroad track and several bridges, completely cutting off the Federal garrison in Chattanooga from its source of rations and almost forcing the Union Army into surrender. The following August, he also succeeded in cutting part of Gen. William T. Sherman's supply lines during the Union commander's Atlanta campaign.

After the fall of Atlanta in September 1864, Wheeler's troopers were detailed along with William Hardee's infantry to stop Sherman's March to the Sea. Wheeler, like Hardee, did his best, but his forces were rather ineffective in light of Sherman's superior numbers. In appreciation of his efforts, however, the Confederate government promoted Fighting Joe to lieutenant general on February 18, 1865.

Wheeler continued resisting Sherman's advance through the Carolinas until Gen.

Maj. Gen. Joseph Wheeler, U.S.A., during the Spanish-American War. **The appointment of the 62-year-old former Confederate general to U.S. Army command was seen as an important gesture of reconciliation between North and South.**

Joseph E. Johnston's surrender on April 26. He was finally captured near Atlanta in May, and held as a prisoner of war until June 8. After his release he became a merchant in New Orleans and then a cotton planter in Wheeler, Alabama, the town which is named in his honor.

Fighting Joe eventually became a lawyer and entered politics, serving as a representative in Congress from 1883 to 1900. At the outbreak of the Spanish-American War in 1898 he offered his services to the government and was commissioned a major general of volunteers by President William McKinley in what was seen as an important gesture of reconciliation between North and South. After serving at San Juan Hill and Santiago, Cuba, he was detailed to the Philippines, returning to the United States early in 1900. Wheeler was subsequently commissioned a brigadier general in the regular Army on June 16. He died in Brooklyn, New York, on January 25, 1906, and is buried in Arlington National Cemetery.

SECRETARY OF STATE
Judah Philip Benjamin   *1811 – 1884*

Judah Benjamin is undoubtedly the most remarkable of the Confederacy's leaders. Although a foreign-born Jew in a largely xenophobic South, Benjamin rose to become Jefferson Davis's secretary of state and was widely hailed as "the brains of the Confederacy."

Judah was born in Saint Croix, British West Indies, on August 6, 1811, the descendant of English and Dutch Sephardic Jews. When he was two, his family moved to America, settling first in Fayetteville, North Carolina, and then in Charleston, South Carolina, where Judah spent his formative years. After attending Yale University for two years, Benjamin went to New Orleans in 1828, where he was hired as a clerk in a law office. In just four years he mastered the intricacies of Louisiana's Napoleonic Code and was admitted to the bar in 1832.

During the time Benjamin was studying law, he earned extra money by tutoring local Creole students in English. One of them, Natalie St. Martin, took a special interest in her teacher and they married in 1833. The match proved to be an unhappy one, however, and in 1845 Natalie Benjamin and her only child, Ninette, left Judah and moved to Paris. He visited them in France regularly for the rest of his life, but they only returned to America once.

Benjamin became a successful lawyer, purchasing a large plantation, Bellechasse, and entering politics. In 1852 he was elected to the U.S. Senate—the first Jewish senator in American history—and became a leading spokesman for Southern rights. After South Carolina left the Union in December 1860, he delivered a stirring oration in the Senate defending secession; and when Louisiana seceded the following February, he resigned his seat in Congress and returned to New Orleans to serve the South.

Benjamin was soon named the Confederacy's first attorney general by President

Judah P. Benjamin, the first Jewish U.S. senator and the Confederate secretary of state. **Known for his inscrutable smile, Benjamin was called "the Sphinx."**

Davis. The choice was not surprising; not only was Judah probably the best lawyer in the South, he was a close friend of Davis as well. The two had met while serving together in the U.S. Senate and became friends after Benjamin challenged Davis to a duel over an alleged insult and Davis respectfully apologized.

Judah Benjamin's tenure as attorney general lasted only a few months. When it became apparent after the First Battle of Bull Run that the war would not be ended quickly, President Davis felt he needed a stronger secretary of war than his initial choice, Leroy Walker. The Confederate President saw his worldly, intelligent attorney general as an ideal man for the job despite Benjamin's lack of military training and appointed him to the post on September 17.

(above) *The cabinet of the Confederate States of America at mid-war.* Judah Benjamin, Jefferson Davis's closest advisor, is seated to the left of the President.

(right) *Jefferson Davis bidding farewell to his escort in Washington, Georgia, on May 3, 1865.* Benjamin, the bearded figure to Davis's right, escaped from here disguised as a visiting Frenchman named Bonfals—French for "good disguise."

Benjamin in his court regalia as Queens Counsel in 1883. The former Confederate attorney general became one of England's finest solicitors after the war.

Unfortunately, the position quickly turned into the low point of Judah's career. In 1861, before ordnance chief Josiah Gorgas had developed an adequate system of supply, the South was ill equipped to fight a national war. Benjamin was unfairly blamed for these problems, the victim of anti-Semitic Confederates who branded him "Davis's pet Jew." After the Confederate loss of Roanoke Island, North Carolina, and the fall of Forts Henry and Donelson in February 1862, the clamor for Judah's dismissal reached a peak, and the Confederate Congress mounted an investigation of his actions as secretary of war. President Davis, fearful that his friend would be made the scapegoat for the war's failures, appointed him Confederate secretary of state on March 17, before the congressional investigation could be finished.

Benjamin remained secretary of state for the rest of the war, directing the South's efforts at foreign recognition and serving as President Davis's most trusted adviser, earning his reputation as the "brains of the Confederacy." After the fall of Richmond on April 2, 1865, Benjamin accompanied Davis on his flight south and took part in the final meeting of the Confederate cabinet at Greensboro, North Carolina, which authorized Gen. Joseph E. Johnston to surrender. Following the South's defeat, Benjamin made his way to the coast, eventually sailing to England, where he claimed citizenship by virtue of his birth in British territory.

Benjamin entered the bar in London in 1866 and became one of the leading lawyers in England. After serving as a Queens Counsel for many years, he retired from practice in 1883. Judah Benjamin died on May 6, 1884, in Paris, France, while visiting his wife.

John Bell Hood   1831 – 1879

John Hood lays a strong claim to being the toughest general in the Confederate Army. An aggressive fighter, he served throughout the war despite the loss of both an arm and a leg, eventually rising to the Confederacy's highest rank of full general.

Hood was born at Owingsville, Kentucky, on June 1, 1831, the son of Dr. John Hood. Inspired by his grandfather's stories of fighting Indians, Hood decided upon a military career and was admitted to West Point in 1849 through the influence of his uncle, Congressman Richard French. A poor student, young John finished near the bottom of his class in 1853.

Appointed a second lieutenant of the infantry, Hood was stationed in California for two years until he was transferred to the 2nd U.S. Cavalry in Texas in 1855. Serving under Colonels Albert S. Johnston and Robert E. Lee, Hood quickly proved himself a tough,

effective officer despite his poor standing at the Military Academy. During a scouting expedition in July 1857, however, he was wounded so badly that he was excused from duty for two years. Still, he didn't resign. Rather, he rejoined his unit as soon as he could, revealing a dedication that would be seen again and again during the Civil War.

Hood left the U.S. Army in favor of the Confederacy on April 17, 1861. Sent to Virginia, he was initially commissioned a lieutenant of cavalry, but by October 1 his obvious leadership capabilities led to his appointment as colonel of the 4th Texas Infantry. Within months he was given command of a brigade—"Hood's Texas Brigade," which comprised the 1st, 4th, and 5th Texas Infantry as well as units from Georgia, South Carolina, and Arkansas—and on March 6, 1862, he was promoted to brigadier general.

General Hood first demonstrated his ag-

gressive fighting style during the Peninsular campaign of 1862. At Eltham's Landing on May 7, for example, his brigade drove back a Union assault from the York River, and at the Battle of Gaines' Mill on June 27 he led his troops in a daring charge that broke a seemingly unassailable Federal line.

Following his triumphs on the Peninsula Hood was assigned command of a division in Gen. James Longstreet's corps of the Army of Northern Virginia, and he played a major role in Longstreet's rout of the Union forces at Second Bull Run on August 30. At the Battle of Antietam on September 17, Hood's troops repulsed numerous Yankee assaults in heavy fighting around the Dunker Church. Although they sustained almost 50 percent casualties, Hood's men held their position throughout the day, helping to secure the northern end of the battlefield for the South. Hood was awarded a major general's commission on October 10.

After Antietam, Gen. Hood did not see much combat until the Gettysburg campaign the following summer (his troops were unused at Fredericksburg and were south with Longstreet during Chancellorsville). On the second day of the Battle of Gettysburg, July 2, 1863, Hood's division spearheaded the Confederate attack against the Federal left flank at Big Round Top and Devil's Den. While directing his troop placements near Plum Run Valley, Hood was severely wounded in his left arm by an artillery shell and removed from the field; historians still speculate that the battle might have ended differently had he not been hit.

(opposite) John Hood's flowing beard and sad-eyed expression made him look much older than he was; during the war he was only in his thirties.

(left) An artist's conception of the brutal fighting at the Second Battle of Bull Run. Hood's troops took a major role in the rout of General Pope's Yankees on the second day of the battle.

(left) *The Dunker Church at Antietam, scene of some of the heaviest fighting at that sanguinary battle.* Hood's troops suffered almost 50 percent casualties here.

(below) *The Devil's Den at Gettysburg.* General Hood's left arm was permanently paralyzed by a wound he received near this position while attacking the Unon left flank on July 2, 1863.

General Hood's injuries were serious—the arm remained crippled for the rest of his life—but not life threatening, and he was able to rejoin Longstreet's corps when it was transferred to Tennessee in September. At the Battle of Chickamauga on the 19th and 20th, he was again badly wounded. This time, he lost his right leg.

Hood, promoted to lieutenant general, returned to the field in February 1864 when he was given command of a corps in Gen. Joseph E. Johnston's Atlanta campaign. When Johnston failed to halt Gen. William T. Sherman's advance southward, he was replaced by Hood, who was awarded the temporary rank of full general. Although he was badly outnumbered by Sherman's Yankees, Hood typically went on the offensive, battling the Union forces on the outskirts of Atlanta until September 1, when he was forced to evacuate the city or face capture. Hood then attempted to lure Sherman away from Georgia by swinging northwest into Tennessee, a desperate gamble that ended in failure when his army was destroyed by a Federal force twice his size at Nashville on December 16. Assuming responsibility for the defeat, Hood resigned his position as general on January 23, 1865, reverting to the rank of lieutenant general. He was on his way to a new assignment in the West when he heard that the war was over and surrendered at Natchez, Mississippi, on May 31.

After the war John Hood settled in New Orleans, where he married and became a successful merchant. He died there on August 30, 1879, during a yellow fever epidemic that also killed his wife and oldest daughter.

CITIZEN VOLUNTEER
Edmund Ruffin 1794 – 1865

Today, 125 years after his death, Edmund Ruffin remains one of the most enduring symbols of the Old South. An ardent secessionist, he gained immortality as the man who fired the first shot of the War Between the States.

Edmund Ruffin was born on January 5, 1794, in Prince George County in Virginia's Tidewater region. After briefly attending William and Mary College in Williamsburg and serving in the War of 1812, Ruffin inherited his father's plantation and settled down to the life of a gentleman farmer.

Ruffin soon discovered that his lands, like those of his neighbors, had been so exploited over the previous 200 years that they were almost useless for growing crops. The inventive young man tried rejuvenating his soil with mixtures of fertilizer and marl (a form of lime), and soon his lands were productive again. His techniques became widely accepted and Ruffin was hailed as the savior of both the Tidewater's plantation agriculture and the system of slavery that accompanied it.

With his farm once again productive, Edmund had time to turn to politics. He became increasingly involved in the controversies over slavery and states' rights, and in the 1850s actively advocated secession as the solution to the South's problems. When South Carolina called its convention of secession in December 1860, Ruffin rushed to Charleston to witness the historic event, and he was jubilant when the state voted to dissolve its links with the United States on December 20. The old man then continued south to Tallahassee, where he addressed Florida secessionists as a self-appointed ambassador of disunion.

Ruffin cut short his travels to return to Charleston when he heard that the Federal garrison there refused to surrender Fort Sumter to state authorities; the fiery old secessionist felt that war might break out at Sumter, and he wanted to be there if it did.

Edmund Ruffin in the uniform of the Palmetto Guards. **Following the bombardment of Fort Sumter there was a great demand for his picture throughout the South, and he posed for several photographers.**

When it became apparent that the South would take military action against Sumter in April, Ruffin decided he could not remain a mere spectator. He quickly enlisted in the Palmetto Guards, a South Carolina militia unit manning one of the Confederate artillery pieces aimed at Sumter. When the bombardment of the fort began at 4:30 A.M. on April 12, the unit allowed its distinguished new recruit the honor of shooting first. Ruffin soon became known as the man who fired the first shot of the war—a claim which, in fact, may or may not have been true, as several artillery batteries fired at 4:30 that morning. Nevertheless, the colorful old man became a powerful symbol of bold defiance for Southerners and of rebel fanaticism for Northerners.

Following the fall of Sumter, Ruffin went back to Virginia. Volunteering for service once again at the First Battle of Bull Run on July 21, 1861, he linked up with another artillery unit, Capt. Delaware Kemper's Alexandria Battery. This time, Ruffin fired one of the last shots of the battle, a well-placed shell that blocked the bridge being used by the retreating Federal troops.

After First Bull Run, Ruffin realized that he was too old to continue fighting with the troops and returned to his plantation, where he remained until the end of the war. On June 18, 1865, he committed suicide, declaring that he could not, as he described it, outlive the liberties of his country. Vitriolic to the last, he left behind a note proclaiming his eternal hatred of "the perfidious, malignant, and vile Yankee race."

LIEUTENANT GENERAL
Jubal Anderson Early   1816 – 1894

Jubal Early was one of the Confederacy's most colorful generals. Gruff, irreverent, and hard drinking, he was clearly not in the chivalrous tradition that bred Jeb Stuart or Robert E. Lee. Still, Early proved himself a dependable field commander at every major battle in the east from First Bull Run to Spotsylvania, and in 1864 he earned his place in history by leading the last major Confederate foray into the North.

Jubal was born in Franklin County, Virginia, on November 3, 1816. After graduating from West Point in 1837 he served briefly in Florida, resigning in 1838 to study law. Admitted to the bar in 1840, he established a practice at Rocky Mount, Virginia, and was elected to a term in the state legisla-

ture. Following service in the Mexican War, Early returned to Rocky Mount, where he remained until the onset of the Civil War.

Although he opposed secession, once Virginia left the Union "Old Jube," like many other loyal Southerners, quickly pledged his support to the Confederacy. Commissioned colonel of the 24th Virginia Infantry, he earned a promotion to brigadier general at the First Battle of Bull Run on July 21. The following spring he was wounded while leading his troops at the Battle of Williamsburg in Virginia.

Recovering in time to take part in the Second Bull Run campaign in August 1862, Early temporarily succeeded to the command of Gen. Richard S. Ewell's division after

Ewell was wounded. At the Battle of Antietam on September 17, Early led Ewell's troops in the battlefield's West Woods area, holding his position against repeated Union assaults. That December Jube played a pivotal role at Fredericksburg by reinforcing the right wing of the Confederate Army in

(opposite) With his bristling beard and piercing eyes, "Old Jube" was one of the South's most colorful generals.

(below) A Union assault at the Battle of Antietam, September 17, 1862. During this bloodiest day in American history Early commanded the Confederate troops at the battlefield's West Woods.

146

the time Jube's troops reached Washington on the 11th, the city was too heavily reinforced to attack, but he had the satisfaction of knowing that he had disrupted Federal operations at Petersburg as planned and boasted that "we haven't taken Washington but we've scared Abe Lincoln like hell!"

Retreating from Washington, Jube's troops swung back into Virginia and then northward into Maryland again, raiding several towns and destroying the home of Federal Postmaster General Montgomery Blair. After burning Chambersburg, Pennsylvania, on July 30 when its citizens refused to pay a $500,000 ransom, Early returned to the Shenandoah Valley, where he remained a serious threat to the North. Badly embarrassed by Early's raids, the Lincoln administration dispatched 48,000 troops under Gen. Philip H. Sheridan to the valley to combat him. After a series of Confederate defeats, Old Jube led a brilliant and audacious counterattack on Sheridan's camp at Cedar Creek on October 19, routing the Yankees. Sheridan soon rallied his troops, however, and drove Early southward, securing the valley for the Union. Following this retreat, most of Early's troops were transferred to Petersburg. Jube remained in the Shenandoah Valley with a small force until March 1865, when virtually his entire command was captured by Gen. George A. Custer at the Battle of Waynesboro.

After Lee's surrender in April, Early donned a disguise and attempted to join the last remaining Confederate troops west of the Mississippi. On hearing that they, too, had surrendered he made his way to Mexico and, from there, to Canada. Returning to the United States in 1869, he spent his last years practicing law and running the Louisiana state lottery. He died in Lynchburg, Virginia, on March 2, 1894.

time to drive off a heavy Federal assault, thereby earning his promotion to major general.

Early continued to add to his successes in the years that followed. He led the final assault at the four-day Battle of Chancellorsville in May 1863, outflanking and driving off the Federal troops under Gen. John Sedgwick at Salem Church. Two months later, in Gettysburg, it was Jube's command that routed the Union's 11th Corps north of town on the first day of the battle. After further service at the Wilderness and Spotsylvania in May 1864, Early was promoted to the rank of lieutenant general.

Early was then transferred to Virginia's Shenandoah Valley, where he organized one of the most daring operations of the war. After routing the Union forces occupying the Valley at Lynchburg on June 18, Early turned his force of 14,000 northward, hoping to distract the Federal high command from their operations around Richmond and Petersburg. By early July, Old Jube's Confederates had occupied Hagerstown and Frederick, Maryland, which they held for $220,000 ransom. After throwing back pursuing Federal troops at the Battle of Monocacy in Maryland on July 9, Early marched on toward Washington, D.C., sending the capital into a panic and forcing the War Department to send additional troops against him from the siege lines at Petersburg. By

Wade Hampton   1818 – 1902

Although he is not well known today, Wade Hampton deserves a place in any study of wartime heroes of the South. One of the richest men in the Confederacy, Hampton risked his fortune to support the South's war effort. An excellent horseman, he became one of the Confederacy's leading cavalry officers and despite the lack of formal military training, succeeded to Gen. Jeb Stuart's command after Stuart's death.

Wade Hampton was born in Charleston, South Carolina, on March 28, 1818, the son of wealthy planter Wade Hampton, Jr. After graduating from South Carolina College in 1836, young Wade assumed the management of his father's plantations in South Carolina and Mississippi, building a considerable fortune in cotton and race horses.

When South Carolina seceded in December 1860, Hampton offered his cotton to the state to use in trade for arms and personally equipped the Hampton Legion, an independent regiment of infantry, cavalry, and artillery troops. Leading them with distinction at First Bull Run, where he was wounded, and during the Peninsular campaign, where he was again wounded at Seven Pines, Hampton was promoted to brigadier general on May 23, 1862, and assigned to the cavalry.

General Hampton, who had been raised in Virginia's hunt country, was a natural horseman and strategist and was quickly named Gen. Jeb Stuart's second-in-command. After taking part in Stuart's raid on Chambersburg, Pennsylvania, in October 1862, Hampton led a series of independent raids on Union troops near Martinsburg, in Virginia's Shenandoah Valley. His reputation as a fighter continued to grow after he was severely wounded in a charge against Gen. George Armstrong Custer's troopers at Get-

Handsome Wade Hampton risked both his life and his fortune to aid the South during the War Between the States.

(above) Well-equipped Confederate cavalrymen in Virginia in 1862. Hampton personally paid to outfit his troopers.

(right) Wade Hampton's home in Charleston, South Carolina. The building was commandeered as Union Gen. John Logan's headquarters after Charleston was captured in 1865.

tysburg on July 3, 1863. As a result, a month later Hampton was promoted to major general of cavalry.

Wade Hampton remained Stuart's second-in-command through the Wilderness campaign, until Jeb's death in May 1864. Succeeding to command of the Cavalry Corps at the opening of the Union siege of Petersburg, Virginia, Wade found himself responsible for repelling Union cavalry attacks that threatened to cut off Richmond and Petersburg from the rest of the Confederacy. Hampton did a remarkable job despite a

The site of Joseph Johnston's surrender at Durham Station, North Carolina. While Johnston and William T. Sherman discussed terms inside the house, General Hampton (bearded officer, right center) and his staff swapped stories with Gen. Judson Kilpatrick's Union cavalrymen outside.

severe lack of horses that forced many of his troops to fight dismounted. At Trevilian Station on June 11 and 12, he not only drove back a force under Gen. Philip H. Sheridan but managed to capture several hundred prisoners and George Custer's headquarters wagon as well. In September he audaciously raided a Federal cattle yard at Coggin's Point, Virginia, returning to Petersburg with 2,500 head of cattle for Lee's starving army.

In January 1865 the Cavalry Corps' lack of horses became critical, and Hampton took part of his command from Petersburg to secure mounts. Before they could return, on February 15, Hampton was promoted to lieutenant general and ordered to South Carolina to cover the retreat of Gen. Joseph E. Johnston's army into North Carolina. When Johnston surrendered to Gen. William T. Sherman on April 26, Hampton felt his command was not bound by the agreement and attempted to link up with the fleeing Confederate President Jefferson Davis. Unable to connect with Davis, and unwilling to capitulate, Hampton disbanded his command and made his way back to his plantation in South Carolina.

Following the war, Hampton worked at rebuilding his holdings in Mississippi and South Carolina. After successfully reestablishing himself, his interests turned to politics. Opposing the radical Republican schemes for Reconstruction in South Carolina, Hampton was elected the state's first postwar Democratic governor in 1876. Reelected in 1878, he resigned to become a U.S. senator, a position he held until 1891. Wade Hampton died at Columbia, South Carolina, on April 11, 1902.

GENERAL
Robert Edward Lee   1807 – 1870

General Lee on Traveller, the beloved horse that carried him throughout the war.

In many ways, Robert E. Lee *was* the Confederacy. More than anyone else, he embodied the chivalry and dedication to duty which have come to symbolize the South's Lost Cause. And while leaders like Jefferson Davis and Judah P. Benjamin were struggling to make the government of the Confederate States of America a reality, it was Lee, one of the true military geniuses of all time, who kept the Confederacy alive for four years with his brilliant victories on the battlefield.

Lee was born to one of Virginia's leading families on January 19, 1807, at Stratford, the family home in Westmoreland County. The son of Revolutionary War hero "Light Horse" Harry Lee, Robert inherited his father's interest in the military. Accepted to West Point in 1825, he displayed a remarkable aptitude for his studies and graduated second in his class in 1829.

Commissioned into the Army's elite Corps of Engineers, Robert E. Lee soon developed a reputation as a precise, efficient officer.

After distinguishing himself as Gen. Winfield Scott's chief engineer during the Mexican War, Lee advanced rapidly, serving as superintendent of the Military Academy at West Point and lieutenant colonel of the 2nd U.S. Cavalry.

(right) A youthful Robert E. Lee as he appeared while serving as superintendent of West Point in the 1850s.

(below) A composite picture of Robert E. Lee and his most important generals. Lee delegated extensive responsibility to his commanders.

Lee first came to national attention in October 1859 during abolitionist John Brown's raid on the Federal arsenal in Harpers Ferry, in what is now West Virginia. On leave in Arlington, Virginia, to take care of his ailing wife—Robert had married Mary Ann Randolph Custis, a great-granddaughter of Martha Washington, in 1831—Colonel Lee was assigned to put down Brown's abortive insurrection, which was intended to start a slave revolt. Commanding a detachment of Marines, Lee captured Brown on October 18, becoming a hero throughout the South.

As the Union's secession crisis developed in 1860, Lee found himself torn between his duty to the Army and his love for Virginia. Although he did not support secession, Lee decided he could never bear arms against the South and turned down an offer to command the armies of the United States on April 18, 1861. On receiving the news that Virginia had seceded the following day, Lee resigned from the U.S. Army and offered his services to the Confederacy.

Lee was commissioned a full general in the Confederate Army and assigned as President Davis's personal military adviser. He remained in this position until Gen. Joseph E. Johnston was wounded during the Peninsular campaign on May 31, 1862. Assuming command of Johnston's forces, which Lee renamed the Army of Northern Virginia, he soon demonstrated the daring, aggressive tactics that would become his hallmark. During the Seven Days' Battles between June 25 and July 1, Lee, with fewer than 65,000 men, drove a Federal Army of more than 100,000 from the outskirts of Richmond, saving the Confederate capital from imminent capture. Lee followed up the Seven Days' Battles with similarly daring victories at the Battles of Cedar Mountain and Second Bull Run in August, earning the respect of his command and the fear of the Northern soldiers who faced him.

Lee—by then known as the "Gray Fox" to both Yankees and Confederates—scored his greatest victory at the Battle of Chancel-

Lee inspired his men unlike any other commander during the war. **Following his surrender, they cheered him in a moving display of undying loyalty and affection.**

lorsville in Virginia in May 1863. Audaciously dividing his forces in the face of a much larger Federal force, Lee totally surprised the Yankees with a flank attack by Stonewall Jackson's troops, driving them off in a rout.

After a year of stunning victories, Lee's luck turned at the Battle of Gettysburg in Pennsylvania, on July 1–3, 1863. Proudly feeling that his Army of Northern Virginia could accomplish anything he asked of it, the Gray Fox lost thousands of men assaulting the heavily defended Union positions on Cemetery Ridge. Following Pickett's famous charge, which ended the battle, Lee realized his mistake and manfully apologized to his shattered troops, saying that he had asked them to do the impossible.

The retreat from Gettysburg in July, 1863. **Before this engagement, Lee's army never lost a battle; after it, they never won one.**

After Gettysburg, Lee went on the defensive, attempting to stem a relentless Federal advance toward Richmond. With his poorly supplied army badly outnumbered by Ulysses S. Grant's Yankees, Lee was forced further and further into Virginia until he was cornered at Petersburg in June 1864. Following a ten-month siege, on April 2, 1865, the Gray Fox was forced to abandon both Petersburg and Richmond. Fleeing westward in an attempt to reach supplies and to join with Joseph Johnston's forces in North Carolina, the famished remnants of Lee's once-proud Army of Northern Virginia were finally trapped at Appomattox Court House, Virginia. There, Robert E. Lee surrendered his troops—and the South's dream of independence—to Ulysses S. Grant on April 9.

After the war Lee lived a quiet life as president of Washington College in Lexington, Virginia—since renamed Washington and Lee University. He died in Lexington on October 12, 1870.

Josiah Gorgas   1818 – 1883

At the beginning of the war the South clearly had the best military leadership, but the North had the advantage in logistics. The man responsible for evening up the odds for the largely agrarian Confederacy was Josiah Gorgas, the chief of ordnance. This inventive officer found solutions for severe problems in manufacturing and supply, providing the South with rifles, cannon, and ammunition throughout the war.

Gorgas was born in Running Pumps, Pennsylvania, on July 1, 1818. The son of a poor farmer, Josiah sought appointment to West Point as the best way for him to acquire both an education and a career. Admitted in 1837, Gorgas graduated sixth in his class in 1841 and was appointed to the Army's highly technical Ordnance Department. Josiah spent the following years studying ordnance in Europe and supervising a number of Army arsenals in the Southern United States.

Gorgas developed many friendships during his service in the South and even married a Southern bride while stationed near Mobile in 1853—Amelia Gayle, daughter of former Alabama Governor John Gayle. When war seemed imminent, Gorgas consequently threw his allegiance to the Confederacy and resigned from the U.S. Army on April 3, 1861.

Commissioned a major in the Confederate Army on April 8, Gorgas was immediately named its chief of ordnance, which made him responsible for arming the entire South. Gorgas found himself facing a Herculean task. Most of the weapons the South had in its arsenals were obsolete smoothbore muskets, some of them ancient flintlocks. There were only about 15,000 serviceable military rifles stockpiled in the whole Confederacy,

and fewer than 1,000 cannon. More significantly, the South did not have a single rifle factory or major source of gunpowder.

Gorgas quickly acted to correct these deficiencies. Using machinery captured at the Federal arsenal at Harpers Ferry, the resourceful major opened rifle factories at Richmond and Fayetteville, North Carolina; by the end of the war he had armories in almost every state in the Confederacy. He developed Richmond's Tredegar Iron Works into a major cannon foundry and established a second one in Macon, Georgia. In little

Josiah Gorgas, the Confederacy's resourceful chief of ordnance.

more than a year gunpowder mills were started and lead mines opened, and by the end of 1862 his ordnance bureau was doing a job that was nothing short of amazing. In recognition of this, Gorgas was promoted several times, finally achieving the rank of brigadier general on November 10, 1864.

In addition to manufacturing arms, Gorgas actively imported them. He sent agents to Europe at the beginning of the war and, with basically no assistance from the Confederate government, kept a string of blockade runners bringing rifles and cannon into the Confederacy as long as Southern ports were open.

Gorgas continued to produce munitions throughout the war, but as the struggle neared its end the Southern railroad system was so badly damaged that he could not get them to troops in the field. When Richmond fell to the Yankees on April 2, 1865, Gorgas destroyed a large stockpile of remaining supplies while his wife and 11-year-old son Billy evacuated their apartment in the arsenal.

After the war Josiah Gorgas moved to Alabama to become manager of the Brierfield Iron Works. After a few years he joined the faculty of the University of the South in Sewanee, Tennessee, and in 1878 was elected president of the University of Alabama. Josiah Gorgas died at Tuscaloosa on May 15, 1883. His son Billy grew up to become Dr. William Crawford Gorgas, the conqueror of yellow fever and future surgeon general of the United States.

Leonidas Polk *1806 – 1864*

To millions of Southerners, the War Between the States was not just a political or economic struggle, it was a holy crusade; a popular Confederate slogan during the war years was "My God first, my country second, and then my family." No one epitomized the Southern belief that God favored their cause better than Leonidas Polk, an Episcopalian bishop who laid down his crozier to become a Confederate general.

Leonidas Polk was born on April 10, 1806, in Raleigh, North Carolina, to a leading family that counted President James K. Polk as a member. After receiving his early education in Raleigh, Leonidas entered the University of North Carolina in 1821 and enrolled at West Point two years later. While a cadet Polk met Jefferson Davis and roomed with Albert Johnston; in his fourth year he became a devout Episcopalian under the tutelage of the Military Academy's new chaplain, Dr. Charles McIlvaine.

After graduating West Point eighth in his class in 1827, Polk resigned his commission after only six months, deciding that his true calling was with his church. He then entered the Virginia Theological Seminary, and was ordained a priest in May 1831. By 1838 he had been elevated to missionary bishop for the Southwestern states, and in 1841 was appointed bishop of Louisiana.

When the war broke out, Jefferson Davis appealed to Polk to temporarily set aside his pastoral duties and accept the field command for which he had been trained at West Point. After deliberating for a few months Polk accepted, and on June 25, 1861, he was commissioned a major general in the Confederate Army. Polk was initially assigned command of the Confederacy's entire western theater of operations, but when his old roommate Albert E. Johnston offered his services to the Confederacy Polk suggested that the more experienced Johnston would be a better choice for commander and stepped aside.

The Confederacy's bishop general, Leonidas Polk.

General Polk remained in the West as one of Johnston's most trusted subordinates. Assigned to protect the central Mississippi River Valley on November 7, Leonidas defeated a Federal assault at Belmont, Missouri, led by a little-known brigadier general named Ulysses S. Grant—making Polk almost the only Southern commander who could claim a victory over the Union Army's future general-in-chief.

Trusting in the Lord for his personal safety, the South's bishop general soon developed a reputation as a fearless fighter. While commanding the center of Johnston's army at the Battle of Shiloh on April 6, 1862, he personally led four assaults near the battlefield's Hornets' Nest. After further hard fighting at Perryville, Kentucky, on October 8 Polk was promoted to lieutenant general and put in charge of a corps in Gen. Braxton

Bragg's Army of Tennessee. At the end of the year he proved his mettle as a corps commander directing the Confederate center at the Battle of Stones River on December 31.

In 1863 Polk accompanied General Bragg's army on its campaign in eastern Tennessee. There, at the Battle of Chickamauga in September, the bishop general made a mistake that would cast a shadow over his entire service to the South. Polk, who was commanding Bragg's right wing, failed to attack the Union lines at dawn on the second day of the battle as he had been ordered to do. Although it seemed to be a simple mixup in orders to his subordinates, Bragg—who did not get along well with Polk (or anyone else for that matter)—removed him from command and threatened to have him courtmartialed. On hearing this, President Davis had Polk reinstated but transferred him to Mississippi to avoid problems with Bragg.

General Polk returned east in May 1864, after Bragg himself had been transferred and replaced by Gen. Joseph E. Johnston. Assigned to support Johnston's campaign to hold back Gen. William T. Sherman's advance on Atlanta, Leonidas Polk was killed by an exploding artillery shell while making a reconnaissance of Sherman's troops at Pine Mountain, Georgia, on June 14, 1864. His loss was mourned by political leaders and churchmen throughout the South.

The Battle of Belmont, Missouri, where General Polk drove off Ulysses S. Grant's Yankees on November 7, 1861.

LIEUTENANT GENERAL

Richard Stoddert Ewell   1817 – 1872

A tough and highly competent professional soldier, Richard Ewell proved to be one of Robert E. Lee's finest generals. Popular among his men and respected by his fellow officers, Ewell's rise to prominence in the Army of Northern Virginia was halted only when serious wounds made further field command impossible.

Dick Ewell was born in the Georgetown district of Washington, D.C., on February 8, 1817, the descendant of an old Virginia family. Appointed to West Point in 1836, he graduated 13 of 42 cadets in 1840 and was assigned to frontier duty in the 1st Dragoons. After extensive service in the Mexican War he was promoted to captain and reassigned to the Southwest, where he gained distinction as an Indian fighter.

Ewell was in the East on leave when the Civil War broke out. Placing his loyalty with Virginia, he resigned his commission in the U.S. Army on May 7, 1861, and was soon appointed a brigadier general in the Confederate infantry.

On first appearance, Ewell did not seem to fit the part of a general. Pop-eyed, with a large nose and bald head—his nickname was "Old Baldy"—Ewell looked more like the caricature of a large bird than a military leader. As if his physiognomy were not enough of a handicap, he also had a lisp that became comically obvious when he was chewing out his troops. Despite these physical drawbacks, he soon proved his abilities as a commander and earned the respect of his men. When he helped to carry the wounded

after one of his first skirmishes and then personally paid a nearby farmer to care for them, any doubts his troops had about Old Baldy disappeared.

Ewell first rose to prominence during Stonewall Jackson's Shenandoah Valley campaign in spring 1862. (Although he was at First Bull Run the previous year, Ewell's unit didn't get into the fight until the battle was almost over.) After helping to drive off

(opposite) Balding and pop-eyed, Richard Ewell's odd appearance belied his effectiveness as a field commander.

(below) The trenches used by Ewell's troops while anchoring the Confederate left during the Battle of the Wilderness. **Today this position is preserved as part of the battlefield park.**

(above) General Ewell's headquarters during the Union siege of Richmond, Virginia.

(right) The surrender of Ewell's badly outnumbered command at Sayler's Creek, Virginia, on April 6, 1865.

View of Fort Warren Boston harbor.

Interior of the Fort.

Gen. Nathaniel Banks's Yankees at the Battle of Winchester on May 25, Old Baldy commanded the Confederate forces that routed Gen. John Frémont's much larger Union Army at the Battle of Cross Keys on June 8. The following day he also played a pivotal role in the Battle of Port Republic, which forced the last remaining Federal troops from the valley.

With the conclusion of the Shenandoah campaign, Ewell's troops saw little action until Jackson's march to Bull Run that summer. During a sharp fight en route, at Groveton, Virginia, on August 28, he was badly wounded in his right knee, necessitating the amputation of his leg. In an interesting comment on medical ethics during the war, one of the doctors who performed the operation was a captured Union surgeon, Dr. James Farley of the 14th Brooklyn militia.

Ewell was on leave for several months following his surgery. During his convalescence the 45-year-old bachelor was cared for by his cousin and childhood sweetheart, Lizinka Campbell Brown, a widow. The experience rekindled their romance, and by the time he had recovered they were married.

Ewell returned to the Army in late May 1863. Promoted to lieutenant general, he was given command of Stonewall Jackson's corps after Jackson's death earlier that month. Ewell left almost immediately on Lee's second northern invasion, the Gettysburg campaign. Old Baldy looked more peculiar than ever strapped into his saddle because of his wooden leg, but he soon proved that he still knew how to fight. Marching through the Shenandoah on his way to Pennsylvania, Ewell surprised a Federal detachment at Winchester, Virginia, on June 14, capturing more than 3,300 Yankees. At the Battle of Gettysburg on July 1–3, Ewell's troops were responsible for the Confederate victory on the first day, breaking the Federal line and driving the Yankees to the outskirts of town.

In the months following Gettysburg it became apparent that General Ewell no

Fort Warren in Boston harbor, where Ewell was imprisoned for three months after his capture at Sayler's Creek.

longer had the stamina for extended field operations. When he was further injured by a fall from his horse at the Battle of Spotsylvania in May 1864, he finally had to be removed from his command. Dick was reassigned to the defenses of Richmond, remaining there until the Confederate capital was abandoned on April 2, 1865. Fleeing the advancing Union army with the rest of Lee's command, Ewell was captured at the Battle of Sayler's Creek on April 6 and was subsequently imprisoned at Fort Warren in Boston harbor.

After his release in July, Richard Ewell moved to a farm near Spring Hill, Tennessee, remaining there until his death on January 25, 1872, just three days after his beloved Lizinka passed away.

Albert Sidney Johnston   1803 – 1862

Albert S. Johnston remains one of the South's most controversial generals—not because of anything he did but because of how he was viewed by others. Considered by many contemporaries to be potentially the Confederacy's finest general—greater even than Robert E. Lee—Johnston died too early in the war for his true place in Confederate history to be assessed.

Albert Johnston was born at Washington, Kentucky, on February 2, 1803. After studies at Transylvania College—where he met Jefferson Davis—Johnston won appointment to West Point in 1822. Graduating with honors in 1826, Albert was assigned to the infantry and served in the Black Hawk War.

Johnston resigned his commission in 1834 to care for his ailing wife. After her death the following year, he moved to the Republic of Texas and enlisted in its army as a private. Rising meteorically when his qualifications became known, Johnston was appointed the senior brigadier general in 1837 and Texas's secretary of war in 1838!

Johnston resigned as war secretary in 1840, but at the outbreak of the Mexican War in 1846 he again offered his services to the Lone Star State and was commissioned colonel of the 1st Texas Rifles. Following the U.S. victory at the Battle of Monterey, Johnston was one of the two officers sent to discuss surrender terms with the Mexicans; the other was the commander of the Mississippi Rifles, Albert's old schoolmate Jefferson Davis.

After the Mexican War Johnston reenlisted in the U.S. Army. Commissioned a colonel, he commanded the 2nd U.S. Cavalry (in which Robert E. Lee served as his second-in-command) and led an expedition into Utah.

Albert Sidney Johnston, the man whom Jefferson Davis regarded as the South's finest general.

In 1860 Johnston was transferred to San Francisco, California, to head the Army's operations on the Pacific Coast. When Texas seceded in February 1861, Johnston followed his adopted state into the Confederacy, resigning his U.S. Army commission as soon as his successor arrived on April 25. Completing a 3,000-mile trek to Richmond, Virginia, on September 6, Johnston was welcomed by his old friend Jeff Davis and immediately commissioned a full general in the Confederate Army.

Johnston was assigned command of the Confederate Department of the West, an impractically large theater of operations that stretched from the Virginia border into Indian territory and from the Gulf of Mexico to Illinois. Establishing his headquarters at Bowling Green, Kentucky, in late October, Johnston started personally recruiting and organizing his troops. As Department commander perhaps he should have delegated more of these duties to others, but Johnston liked to have contact with his men, inspiring them by his leadership rather than directing them from afar.

Johnston's position at Bowling Green was soon threatened by an advancing Union force under Gen. Don Carlos Buell. Unwilling to risk his command against a Federal force

The beginning of the Battle of Shiloh, April 6, 1862. Johnston's dawn attack on the Federal troops (above) completely surprised the Yankees.

outnumbering him two-to-one, Johnston abandoned Bowling Green on February 7, 1862, retreating first to Nashville, Tennessee, and then to Corinth, Mississippi. Johnston's apparent refusal to fight caused many to call for his removal, but he insisted that his troops would engage the enemy when conditions were right for victory, and Jefferson Davis dismissed criticism of his friend with the simple statement, "If Sidney Johnston is not a general, we have no generals."

Conditions became right in late March when a Federal force under Gen. Ulysses S. Grant set up camp near Shiloh, Tennessee, to wait for Buell's troops to join them. Johnston knew that Grant's Yankees were in a poor defensive position on the banks of the Tennessee River and quickly organized an attack, hoping to defeat Grant before Buell could arrive. Totally surprising the Yankees on the morning of April 6, 1862, Johnston's troops came close to winning the Battle of Shiloh before their advance, hindered by Gen. P.G.T. Beauregard's new troop reorganization, was halted near the battlefield's Peach Orchard. Riding there to personally direct the attack, as he liked to do, Albert Sidney Johnston was hit in the leg by a stray bullet and died of loss of blood before medi-

cal help could arrive. After his death the attack foundered, and the next day General Beauregard ordered a retreat back to Corinth.

Today, some 125 years later, the effect that General Johnston might have had at Shiloh—and at future battles—had he survived remains one of the great unanswered questions of the Confederacy.

CAPTAIN
Sally Tompkins   *1833 – 1916*

In a rebel army of more than a million men, Sally Tompkins was unique. Possibly the finest hospital administrator in the South, this plucky lady was the one and only woman commissioned an officer by the Confederate States of America.

Sally was born at her family home, Poplar Grove, in Matthews County, Virginia, on November 9, 1833. After her father's death, her mother moved the family to Richmond, where Sally became active in charities and church work.

At the beginning of the war neither the Union nor the Confederacy had established an adequate system of field hospitals. Following the First Battle of Bull Run on July 21, 1861, the Confederate government found itself unable to care for the more than 1,500 soldiers wounded in that action and put out a call for civilians to assist with their care. Responding to this call, Sally received permission from a family friend, Judge John Robertson, to use his large home in Richmond as a hospital. Equipping it herself, Miss Tompkins opened Robertson Hospital on August 1 and—although she had no formal training as a nurse—soon developed it into one of the best aid stations in Richmond.

"Captain Sally" Tompkins, supervisor of Richmond's Robertson Hospital, and the only woman to hold a military commission from the Confederacy.

When the Confederacy began organizing its military hospital system that September, the government declared that all such facilities had to be under the control of the Army. In order to keep Robertson's highly efficient supervisor, Confederate President Jefferson Davis issued Sally a commission as a captain in the cavalry. The commission allowed "Captain Sally," as she was known for the rest of her life, to draw provisions and issue orders to soldiers on her staff. Tompkins returned her pay to the government, continuing to use her own funds for items not available through the War Department.

Captain Sally compiled a remarkable record in her four years at Robertson Hospital. Working at a time before the acceptance of germ theory when secondary infections killed hundreds of thousands of wounded soldiers, she and her nurses lost only 73 out of 1,333 patients—the finest record of any hospital in the Confederacy despite the fact that Robertson regularly received many of the worst-injured soldiers in Richmond. This phenomenal success rate can only be attributed to the care which Captain Sally demanded for her boys, keeping them constantly clean, well fed, and in good spirits.

Sally Tompkins, like Phoebe Pember, continued to care for her patients even after the fall of Richmond to Federal forces on April 2, 1865. When the hospital closed on June 13, she returned to her home in Richmond and continued with her charitable activities for as long as she was able. Eventually becoming destitute herself, Sally spent her last years in the Home for Confederate Women in Richmond. Captain Sally died there on July 25, 1916, and was buried in Richmond with full military honors.

One of the many small hospital wards established early in the war in hotels and private residences. The hospital in Judge Robertson's home would have looked much like this.

Lewis Addison Armistead   1817 – 1863

When most people think of the epic charge at Gettysburg that was the high-water mark of the Confederacy, they usually think of Gen. George E. Pickett. But it was actually Gen. Lewis Armistead who led the assault that broke through the Union defenses on Cemetery Ridge. Armistead perished in the attack, a hero to the South.

Lewis Armistead was born in New Bern, North Carolina, on February 18, 1817, the son of Col. Walker Armistead, a career U.S. Army officer. Following in his father's footsteps, Lewis was appointed to West Point in 1834, but he was dismissed in 1836 after a mess-hall fight in which he broke a plate over the head of fellow cadet Jubal Early, a future Confederate general. Despite this mishap, Armistead was commissioned a second lieutenant in the 6th U.S. Infantry in 1839. He served in the Seminole War and the Mexican War, and on the Pacific Coast, earning along the way his nickname "Lo," short for Lothario. Particularly popular with the ladies, who liked his quiet, gentlemanly demeanor, Armistead was married twice.

When the Civil War broke out Lo, by then a captain, was posted in California. Like many of his fellow officers—including the U.S. Army commander in the Far West, Col. Albert S. Johnston—Lewis was torn between his duty to the Army and his loyalty to his home state. Finally he resigned his commission to go with the South. The difficulty of this decision surfaced at a farewell reception held for the departing Southern officers at Army headquarters in Los Angeles in May 1861. Toward the end of the evening Mrs. Albert Johnston sat down at the piano and led the group in singing "Kathleen Mavourneen," a sentimental ballad about parting that was popular at the time. The song ends as the lovers vow to see each other again although "it may be for years, and it may be forever." Recognizing a prophetic note in this lament over the separation of

This wartime engraving gives testament to Lewis Armistead's rugged good looks. He was nicknamed "Lothario."

loved ones, Armistead turned to his Northern friend Capt. Winfield Scott Hancock and, with tears in his eyes, said "Hancock . . . you can never know what this has cost me."

After making his way east, Armistead was appointed Colonel of the 57th Virginia Infantry. He was promoted to brigadier general on April 1, 1862, and placed in command of a brigade in General Pickett's division. In June of that year Lo soon distinguished himself as an effective field commander during the Peninsular campaign's Battle of Seven

Pines and the Seven Days' Battles. He followed these engagements with conspicuous service at Second Bull Run and at Antietam, where he was wounded in action.

General Armistead's finest hour came at Gettysburg. On the third day of the battle— July 3, 1863—he spearheaded the attack of Pickett's division against the Federal position on Cemetery Ridge, an assault that has gone down in history as the legendary "Pickett's Charge."

The fighting opened around 1 P.M. with a massive, two-hour artillery duel between the Union and Confederate Armies that forced the rebel infantry to lie down out of harm's way. Armistead continued walking among his troops, however, calming and inspiring

them by his example. When some complained that he should not expose himself to such danger, he shrugged off their concerns, saying that an army could afford to lose a general or two before a battle but it could not afford to lose a single fighting man.

The charge began about 3 P.M., after the artillery duel had ceased. Armistead commanded the troops attacking the center of the Federal line, a position defended by his old comrade Winfield Scott Hancock, now a Union general. Armistead focused his assault on a cluster of chestnut oaks—the Gettysburg battlefield's famous "Copse of Trees"—behind a low stone wall a mile east of the Confederate lines.

The general placed his hat on the tip of his outstretched sword as a rallying point and led his troops toward the copse through a murderous volley of Yankee rifle and cannon fire. Only about 300 men made it to the wall with him, but Armistead urged them on with the cry, "Come on boys! Give them cold steel!" As he commanded, the Confederates fixed bayonets and fought their way across the wall in brutal hand-to-hand combat, but they were quickly outnumbered and driven off. Armistead himself was cut down by a Yankee bullet just as he reached the Federal artillery in the copse. Mortally wounded, he requested that his personal effects be given to his old friend Hancock.

Lewis Armistead died in a Union field hospital in Gettysburg on July 5, 1863. His body was subsequently interred in St. Paul's Churchyard in Baltimore, Maryland.

Nathan Bedford Forrest 1821 – 1877

Nathan Forrest may have been the Confederacy's most brilliant commander. A natural leader and tactician, Forrest achieved a remarkable record of successes although he had no formal military training and lacked the breadth of experience borne by the South's other leading generals.

Forrest was born on July 13, 1821, in Bedford County (now Marshall County), Tennessee, the eldest son of William and Mariam Forrest. After his father's death in 1837 the 16-year-old Nathan assumed responsibility for his large family, then living in Mississippi. With almost no formal education, he worked his way from a farm laborer to a horse dealer and slave trader, eventually purchasing several cotton plantations and amassing a fortune of more than $1 million. He returned to Tennessee in 1849, settling in Memphis, where he became a leading citizen and alderman.

At the beginning of the Civil War, Forrest volunteered as a private in a local cavalry company, but at the request of Tennessee's governor he subsequently raised and equipped a cavalry battalion of his own and was commissioned its commander in October with the rank of lieutenant colonel. His first assignment was the defense of Fort Donelson, Tennessee, in February 1862. Disgusted at the unwillingness of Donelson's commander John Floyd to fight Gen. Ulysses S. Grant's Yankees, he led his troopers to safety across the freezing Cumberland River, practically the only commander at Donelson to escape Grant's demand of "unconditional surrender" on February 16.

Promoted to colonel, Forrest next took part in the Battle of Shiloh in April, where he was severely wounded while his troopers acted as the retreating rebels' rear guard. On his recovery in July, he was named brigadier general and assigned to lead his cavalry troops in a series of raids on Union Army positions in Tennessee. Moving out of Chattanooga on July 6, he soon revealed himself to be a superb tactician and daring fighter when his men captured an entire Union brigade and supplies worth more than a million dollars at Murfreesboro. Other triumphs emerged over the next several months as Forrest led similar raids on Federal garrisons and cavalry units throughout Tennessee.

It is said that Forrest once summed up his approach to fighting with the dictum "Git thar fust with the most men," but his real genius lay in his repeated ability to win even when he was outnumbered. Nowhere was this skill more apparent than in his victory over a Union cavalry force under Col. Abel Streight in spring 1863. After leading

(right) Forrest's remarkable victory at Brice's Crossroads is commemorated by this impressive monument at the site of the battle.

(opposite) Nathan B. Forrest, one of the South's most outstanding cavalry officers.

Streight's Yankees on a 150-mile chase, Forrest bluffed the 1,500 Federal soldiers into thinking they were outnumbered and they surrendered to his command of 500 exhausted troopers—a remarkable feat unequaled in the annals of the Civil War.

In summer 1863, General Forrest moved his force into southeastern Tennessee to take part in Gen. Braxton Bragg's Chickamauga campaign. He played a minor role in the battle itself, but afterward he led his cavalry to Chattanooga in pursuit of the retreating Yankees, urging Bragg to attack. When Bragg allowed the Union forces to escape, Forrest became irate and engaged in a heated

fight with his commander. Forrest was subsequently transferred by President Davis to restore peace.

In spring 1864 Forrest, by then promoted to major general, resumed his audacious raids through central Tennessee and Kentucky. Gen. William T. Sherman dispatched a force of 8,000 Union soldiers to stop the man he called "that devil Forrest," but the heavily outnumbered Confederate general decisively defeated the Yankees in another brilliant victory at the Battle of Brice's Crossroads in Mississippi on June 10. Forrest continued his crippling strikes against Federal installations in Tennessee and Alabama for the remainder of the war, finally rising to the rank of lieutenant general on February 28,

The Battle of Brice's Crossroads, Mississippi.
Here, on June 10, 1864, Forrest defeated a Federal force outnumbering him three to one, a feat unequalled during the war.

1865. After Gen. Joseph E. Johnston's surrender on April 26, there was fear that Forrest would continue a guerrilla war in the West, but he surrendered quietly on May 4 after instructing his men to go home, "be good citizens and obey the laws."

After the war Nathan Forrest returned to Tennessee to rebuild his fortune. He died in Memphis on October 29, 1877.

Jefferson Davis   1808 – 1889

No single individual did more to establish the Confederacy than did its first and only President, Jefferson Davis. Although he never sought the office, once appointed he worked at it tirelessly, managing to hold the fledgling nation together for four years in the face of almost insurmountable difficulties.

Jefferson Davis was born in Christian County, Kentucky, on June 3, 1808, and raised in Mississippi. After studies at St. Thomas's College and Transylvania College, in Kentucky, he was appointed to West Point, graduating 23 out of 32 cadets in 1828. Jefferson served in various posts in the Indian Territories until 1835 when he resigned his commission and eloped with the daughter of his commander, Col. (later President) Zachary Taylor.

Davis moved to Mississippi and bought a plantation, but his happiness was cut short by the death of his wife just three months after their marriage. He spent the following years developing his farm and nurturing a growing interest in politics, and in 1845 he was elected to Congress. He also married for the second time, wedding 19-year-old Varina Howell in February of that year.

Jeff Davis resigned his seat in Congress at the outbreak of the Mexican War the following June to command the Mississippi Rifles. Their stand at the Battle of Buena Vista won the battle for the United States and made Davis a war hero, greatly boosting his political career. Within a matter of months he was appointed U.S. senator from Mississippi. Then, after President Franklin Pierce's election in 1852, he was named secretary of war.

At the close of the Pierce administration in 1857 Jeff Davis was reappointed to the Senate, where he became a leading spokesman for the rights of the slave states. When Abraham Lincoln was elected President on a platform limiting the extension of slavery, Davis, like many Southern leaders, saw no

Jefferson Davis, Mexican War hero and U.S. senator, in 1849.

Davis as President of the Confederate States of America. **The strain of the office is evident in his features.**

that, on receiving the news, "he looked so grieved that I feared some evil had befallen our family." Jeff Davis, who was chosen as the most experienced man the South had for the job, felt duty-bound to accept the post and was inaugurated on February 18.

The new President found himself faced with almost impossible tasks. He had to practically create a nation, overseeing every government function—from seeking foreign recognition to establishing a postal system. Above and beyond this, he had to direct the Confederacy's war effort, dealing with problems of supply, transportation, communications, and command in a war that stretched from the Atlantic coast to New Mexico and Colorado. Rising to the challenge, Davis drove himself mercilessly, often to the point of collapse, and accomplished as much as

alternative to secession. After Mississippi voted to leave the Union on January 9, 1861, Jeff Davis made an emotional farewell speech in the Senate and returned to his plantation, Brierfield, to prepare for war.

Davis, who had been named commanding general of the Mississippi state forces upon his return from Washington, anticipated that he would receive an important field command from the Confederate legislature then being formed. When he was notified that they had instead selected him as the Confederacy's provisional president he was stunned and disappointed; his wife recalled

Davis's inauguration as provisional President of the Confederacy at the Capitol building in Montgomery, Alabama, February 18, 1861. **After Virginia seceded in April the Confederate capital was moved to Richmond.**

was humanly possible given the Confederacy's limited resources. Ironically, he was often accused of assuming too much power for his central government and infringing upon the rights of the individual Confederate states, the same complaint he had leveled against the Federal government while a senator.

Davis's worst failing as President was, surprisingly, in the crucial area of military affairs. Still longing for field command, he constantly interfered in his generals' decisions and sometimes arrived in the midst of battles to personally direct troop movements. In addition, his strong sense of personal loyalty led him to retain friends in high commands even after they had proven themselves un- qualified. Davis made these decisions with the best interests of the Confederacy at heart, however, and it should be remembered that he made many excellent decisions as well, chief among them his unqualified support for Robert E. Lee.

When the Confederacy reached its final days in April 1865, Davis evacuated the capi- tal city of Richmond with his family and cabinet, heading toward Gen. Joseph E. Johnston's forces in North Carolina. Davis unrealistically believed that the war could

"Davis and his Generals," a composite picture showing many of the Confederacy's impor- tant field commanders. **President Davis took his responsibilities as commander-in-chief literally and often meddled in his generals' decisions.**

still be won, but a conference held with Johnston, P. G. T. Beauregard, and the chief cabinet officers in Greensboro on April 12 convinced him that the fight was over, and he authorized Johnston to surrender. Continuing his flight southward, Jeff Davis was captured by pursuing Federal troops near Irwinville, Georgia, on May 10. When caught he was wearing his wife's cloak, which he had grabbed by accident, leading to the embarrassing rumor that he had attempted to escape disguised as a woman.

Jefferson Davis was confined in the Union prison at Fort Monroe, Virginia, for two years before being released without trial. He returned to Mississippi and died in New Orleans on December 6, 1889, the most enduring symbol of the South's lost cause.

Jefferson Davis shortly before his death in 1889. Like many public officials North and South he suffered the indignity of having his picture used to advertise patent medicine—in this case, **Harter's Iron Tonic.**

LIEUTENANT GENERAL

William Joseph Hardee   1815 – 1873

Next to Robert E. Lee and Stonewall Jackson, William Hardee was possibly the best-known general in the Confederate Army. Hardee's fame did not lay in his victories on the battlefield—although he was a first-rate field commander—but rather in the fact that he authored a little manual that millions of Union and Confederate recruits used to become soldiers, Hardee's *Rifle and Light Infantry Tactics.*

Hardee was born on October 12, 1815, at his family estate, Rural Felicity, in Camden County, Georgia. The son of a former cavalry officer, William was appointed to West Point in 1834 and on his graduation four years later was assigned to the 2nd U.S. Dragoons. Following service in the Seminole War, Hardee decided to make a career of the military and was sent to study cavalry tactics in France. After extensive service in the Mexican War and the 2nd U.S. Cavalry—where he served with such future luminaries as Albert E. Johnston, Robert E. Lee, George H. Thomas, and John Hood—Hardee was ordered by Secretary of War Jefferson Davis to prepare a comprehensive new drill manual for the infantry. Following publication of his *Rifle and Light Infantry Tactics* in 1855, Hardee was promoted to lieutenant colonel and made commandant of cadets at West Point.

Hardee was on leave in Georgia when his home state seceded on January 19, 1861, and he promptly resigned from the U.S. Army. Commissioned a colonel in the Confederate Army, William was assigned to organize a brigade in Arkansas. He was promoted to brigadier general on June 16, 1861. After campaigns in Arkansas and Kentucky, Hardee was commissioned a major general on October 7 and given command of a corps under Gen. Albert S. Johnston. At the Battle of Shiloh the following April, Hardee's corps outshined the rest of Johnston's troops, smashing through the right wing of the

William J. Hardee, the experienced drillmaster and infantry commander known as "Old Reliable."

Union Army and driving off the Yankees in a rout. The action came close to winning the day for the Confederacy and earned Hardee promotion to lieutenant general in October 1862.

After Shiloh, William Hardee—who had deservedly become known as "Old Reliable" among his fellow officers—was assigned to Gen. Braxton Bragg's command. Like many others, he had serious disagreements with Bragg, and after the Battles of Perryville in Kentucky and Stones River in Tennessee later that year, he requested a transfer. Briefly reassigned to Mississippi in mid-1863, Old Reliable was sorely missed at the Battle of Chickamauga in September and was soon ordered back to Bragg's command for the Chattanooga campaign. The importance of Hardee's leadership was confirmed at the Battle of Chattanooga that November when his troops performed well at what was otherwise a Confederate rout. Following Chattanooga, in spring 1864, Hardee's command was assigned to Gen. Joseph E. Johnston's campaign to stop the Federal advance on Atlanta. Johnston's efforts ended

in failure, but as usual Old Reliable's troops fought well, driving off repeated Yankee assaults at Kennesaw Mountain in May and almost defeating Gen. James B. McPherson's troops outside Atlanta in July.

After the fall of Atlanta, Hardee was given the impossible task of stopping Gen. William T. Sherman's march through Georgia and the Carolinas. Hopelessly outnumbered, he was forced to abandon Savannah, Charleston, and Columbia to the advancing Yankees, and by March 1865 had been pushed into North Carolina. Making a final but futile stand at the Battle of Bentonville on March 19, Hardee surrendered his troops to Sherman along with Joseph Johnston's on April 26.

After the war William Hardee settled in Selma, Alabama, serving briefly as the president of the Selma & Meridian Railroad. He died while traveling in Wytheville, Virginia, on November 6, 1873. The book of tactics for which he is best remembered is still widely used, the bible of current-day Civil War reenactors.

Simon Bolivar Buckner   1823 – 1914

Simon Bolivar Buckner is one of those unfortunate figures whose entire careers are overshadowed by one event. A dedicated officer who served bravely in several battles, he is usually remembered solely for his unconditional surrender to Ulysses S. Grant at Fort Donelson.

Buckner was born near Munfordville, Kentucky, on April 1, 1823, and named for Simón Bolívar, the South American patriot. Buckner remained in his native Hart County, Kentucky, until 1840, when he was appointed to West Point. Graduating in 1844, Buckner saw extensive service in the Mexican War as an officer in the 6th U.S. Infantry. After the war he returned to West Point as an infantry instructor. Subsequent to assignments in the Minnesota Territory and in New York, he resigned from the U.S. Army in 1855 to pursue a career in business, finally settling in Louisville, Kentucky, in 1858.

When the Civil War broke out in 1861, Kentucky, a border state, proclaimed its neutrality. Buckner, then a major general in the state militia, was assigned the unenviable job of negotiating the Bluegrass State's neutral status with the surrounding Union and Confederate Armies. When Federal troops reneged on an agreement and marched into Kentucky that June, he lost faith in the Union but scrupulously maintained his own neutrality until the Kentucky legislature declared itself for the North in September. Unwilling to support this decision, he then offered his support to the South. Buckner was immediately commissioned a brigadier general in the Confederate Army and assigned to Gen. Albert S. Johnston's command at Bowling Green, Kentucky.

Gen. Simon Buckner at the beginning of the Civil War. His unusual collar insignia and shoulder boards suggest that what he is wearing is probably a Kentucky state uniform.

(above) A fanciful depiction of the "capture of Fort Donelson" on February 15, 1862. In reality, the fort was forced into surrender, not captured at rifle point.

(right) The Dover Hotel, site of Buckner's "unconditional surrender" to Ulysses S. Grant following the fall of Fort Donelson. The building is now preserved as a museum.

The Confederate line of battle at Chickamauga. **General Buckner commanded one of the first units to break through the center of the Union line on the second day of the fight.**

In February 1862, Johnston, facing a sizable Federal offensive, was forced to abandon Bowling Green and head south. At that time he assigned Buckner and Gen. John Floyd to take 12,000 men and reinforce Fort Donelson, a strategically important Confederate post controlling the Cumberland River on the Tennessee–Kentucky border. Shortly after Buckner and Floyd arrived, the fort was surrounded by Federal gunboats on the river and 25,000 Union troops under Gen. Ulysses S. Grant on the landward side. On February 15, General Floyd inexplicably called off an attempt by Buckner's troops to fight their way past the Yankees, and the rebel garrison was left with no choice but to surrender. Floyd, the senior officer there, promptly turned command over to Gen. Gideon Pillow and snuck out of the fort; Pillow, in turn,

turned command over to Buckner, who alone accepted the responsibility for surrendering. The following morning he asked Grant for his terms and received the now-famous reply that "No terms except unconditional and immediate surrender can be accepted." Grant's harsh demand was galling to Buckner, who had known Ulysses since West Point days and had even given him a loan eight years earlier when Grant was flat broke in New York. However, Buckner realized that it was strictly a military decision and did not hold it against his old friend.

General Buckner was held in Union prisoner of war camps in Indianapolis and Boston for a few months until he was exchanged in August 1862. Returning to field command as a major general, he took part in the Battle of Perryville, in Kentucky, that October and commanded a corps at Chickamauga the following September. After criticizing the

poor leadership of Gen. Braxton Bragg, his commanding officer at Chickamauga, Buckner was subsequently transferred to Louisiana to ease tensions. Promoted to lieutenant general, he remained in Louisiana until the end of the war, finishing his service to the Confederacy by negotiating the surrender of the final rebel troops west of the Mississippi on May 26, 1865.

Buckner made a fortune in real estate after the war and was elected governor of Kentucky in 1887. Retaining his friendship with Grant, he offered to assist the ex-President when he ran into financial troubles and served as a pallbearer at his funeral. Simon Bolivar Buckner died at his estate near Munfordville on January 8, 1914, the last surviving lieutenant general of the Confederacy.

INTELLIGENCE AGENT
Rose O'Neal Greenhow   1817 – 1864

The North displayed a remarkable naiveté about military intelligence at the beginning of the Civil War. Government officials permitted newspapers to print detailed descriptions of troop movements, and they allowed known Southern sympathizers to gather information right in the nation's capital. The best of these Confederate agents in Washington was a 44-year-old widow known as "Rebel Rose"—Rose O'Neal Greenhow.

Rose O'Neal was born in Port Tobacco, Maryland, in 1817. As a young lady she moved to her aunt's boardinghouse in Washington, D.C., where she met many influential government officials, among them John C. Calhoun, who supposedly turned Rose into a partisan of Southern rights. Around 1840 Rose married Dr. Robert Greenhow, a highly respected physician and linguist who was working as a translator in the State Department. Robert, who died in 1854, opened many of Washington's most fashionable circles to Rose, and the charming, intelligent woman became close friends with a number of Washington's leading politicians including James Buchanan, William H. Seward, and Henry Wilson, chairman of the Senate Military Affairs Committee.

When secession became likely following Abraham Lincoln's election in 1860, Mrs. Greenhow was recruited as a spy by Thomas Jordan, a U.S. Army captain with Southern sympathies. Jordan instructed her in how to meet couriers and send secret messages and then left her to use her widespread connections to gather information for the South. She succeeded in getting extensive intelligence about Union troop movements and assignments, passing it along to the Confederacy in ciphered notes.

Mrs. Greenhow's most important contribution to the Confederate cause occurred before the First Battle of Bull Run in July 1861. She kept Gen. P.G.T. Beauregard fully advised as to the number of U.S. soldiers being sent to Virginia, and was able to

Rose O'Neal Greenhow, shown with one of her daughters in the courtyard of the Old Capitol Prison.

warn Gen. Joseph E. Johnston about a Federal plan to cut the vital rail link between Manassas and the Shenandoah Valley. As a result, Johnston was able to keep the railroad open and transport his troops to Bull Run in time to win the battle for the South.

Following First Bull Run, Union officials grew suspicious of Mrs. Greenhow and assigned private detective Allan Pinkerton to keep her under surveillance. After witnessing many Confederate agents calling at her house, Pinkerton arrested Rose on August 23. She was confined to her home—soon known as "Fort Greenhow" because of the heavy guard—but still managed to gather information from visitors and send coded messages in letters. The clever captive even developed a color code to send messages in her needlework!

After five months Greenhow was transferred to the Old Capital Prison in Washington. She was finally released in June 1862 with the promise that she wouldn't return North for the duration of the war. She subsequently sailed to England as a Confederate courier. While returning to the South, her ship ran aground off Wilmington, North Carolina, on October 1, 1864. Mrs. Greenhow attempted to make shore in a lifeboat, but the $2,000 in gold that she was carrying dragged her underwater and she drowned. Rose Greenhow's body was recovered a few days later, and she was buried in Wilmington with full military honors.

James Jay Archer 1817 – 1864

James Archer was among the South's finest brigade commanders. Serving in Gen. A. P. Hill's Light Division, he distinguished himself in many battles of the Army of Northern Virginia, though he was one of the relatively few Confederate generals who had not been trained at West Point.

Archer was born in Bel Air, Maryland, on December 19, 1817. After graduating from Princeton University in 1835, he studied law at the University of Maryland and became a practicing attorney. At the outbreak of the Mexican War in 1846, he volunteered for service and was commissioned a captain in the regular Army. At the close of hostilities in 1848, he returned to his law practice but subsequently reentered the Army in 1855 as captain of the 9th U.S. Infantry.

Captain Archer resigned his position in the U.S. Army at the onset of the Civil War to offer his services to the South. He was commissioned colonel of the 5th Texas Infantry in 1861, and on June 3, 1862, was promoted to brigadier general and given command of a unit in Hill's division known as the Tennessee Brigade (which consisted of some men from Georgia and Alabama as well).

Archer's troops took a conspicuous role in all of the battles in which Hill's division was engaged, starting with the Battle of Beaver Dam Creek, Virginia, on June 26, 1862. At the Battle of Cedar Mountain on August 9, they helped spearhead the Confederate counterattack that broke the Union line, saving the day for the South. Later that month, at the Second Battle of Bull Run, Archer's brigade again distinguished itself, holding off repeated Yankee assaults against the Northern end of the Confederate line until it was reinforced.

Archer's most important service to the Confederacy came at the Battle of Antietam on September 17, 1862. After taking part in Stonewall Jackson's capture of Harpers Ferry

a few days earlier, Archer—along with the rest of Hill's command—arrived at Antietam on the afternoon of the 17th just in time to stop a Union offensive on the south end of the battlefield that threatened to rout Lee's Army of Northern Virginia. Ill and exhausted, Archer directed the attack from an ambulance that carried him to the front.

Although not yet fully recovered from his illness, General Archer also played a promi-

James Archer's penetrating gaze captures the fierce determination of this Confederate general who led assaults at Cedar Mountain, Antietam, and Gettysburg.

nent role at the Battle of Fredericksburg in December, where his men bore the brunt of the Federal assault south of the Virginia town. Under Archer's skillful direction, they again held their line until reinforcements

could be rushed in for a counterattack. The
following spring he further distinguished
himself at the Battle of Chancellorsville,
where his brigade was instrumental in capturing the high open ground at Hazel Grove.
This natural artillery position proved the key
to Southern victory on the third day of the
battle.

Archer's luck turned at Gettysburg, where
his brigade was the first Confederate unit to
enter the battle on July 1, 1863. Moving
eastward into McPherson's Woods, he was
surprised by the Union's Iron Brigade and
more than 1,000 of his men were captured,
including Archer himself, who was uncere-
moniously nabbed by an Irish private. Add-
ing insult to injury, as he was being brought
to the rear, Archer ran into Abner Doubleday, a Federal general whom he had known
before the war. Surprised at seeing his old

friend, Doubleday exclaimed "Archer! I'm
glad to see you!"—to which the captured
Confederate understandably replied, "Well,
I'm not glad to see you by a damn sight."

After Gettysburg, General Archer was
sent to the U.S. Prisoner of War Camp at
Johnson's Island, Ohio. Exchanged a year
later, his health shattered by the poor conditions at Johnson's Island, Archer was ordered
back to his command, then on the siege lines
at Petersburg. Unable to stand the rigors of
trench warfare, General Archer died within
a few months of his release, on October 24,
1864.

*The fighting at Chancellorsville, Virginia, on
May 3, 1863.* **Archer's brigade secured the
strategically important high ground at Hazel
Grove, shown at the left rear, which enabled
Lee's artillery to drive the Yankees from
Chancellorsville.**

Thomas Jonathan Jackson   1824 – 1863

Along with Robert E. Lee, Gen. Thomas "Stonewall" Jackson was one of the two most outstanding strategists of the Confederate Army. Lee's most trusted commander, no other general helped win more decisive victories for the South, and no other commander's death dealt a more serious blow to the Confederacy.

Jackson was born in Clarksburg, in western Virginia, on January 21, 1824. Orphaned at age seven and raised by his uncle, Thomas was a quiet boy who compensated for a lack of natural brilliance by hard work. Appointed to West Point in 1842, he applied himself to his studies with typical energy and four years later, he graduated 17 of 59 cadets.

The newly commissioned Lieutenant Jackson was detailed to artillery service in the Mexican War, where he distinguished himself at the Battle of Chapultepec. After the war he was assigned to posts in New York and Florida, but he resigned his commission in 1851 to become professor of "natural and experimental philosophy" (i.e., science) and artillery tactics at the Virginia Military Institute in Lexington.

Jackson became known as "Tom Fool" among the students at VMI, in response to both his limited knowledge of "natural philosophy" and his personal eccentricities, which included constantly sucking lemons to ease the discomfort of an ulcer. Painfully ill at ease with other people, Jackson was a poor conversationalist and displayed almost no sense of humor; on the few occasions when he found something amusing, he would throw his head back and open his mouth, but never laugh. His sole interests, then and for the rest of his life, were the military and religion (he was a devout Presbyterian).

Jackson remained at VMI until Virginia's secession in April 1861, when he was given

Thomas Jackson before the war, while an instructor at the Virginia Military Institute. **His personal eccentricities led the students to call him "Tom Fool."**

(above) Wilderness Church, Virginia, where Jackson launched his daring surprise attack on the Army of the Potomac during the Battle of Chancellorsville.

Lt. Gen Thomas Jackson, Robert E. Lee's most trusted and brilliant subordinate. His determined gaze reflects his nickname, "Stonewall."

command of the 1st Brigade of Virginia Volunteers—later known as the famous "Stonewall Brigade"—consisting of the 2nd, 4th, 5th, 27th, and 33rd Regiments of Virginia Infantry. While leading these troops at the First Battle of Bull Run, on July 21, 1861, Jackson earned his nickname, "Stonewall." Posted on the battlefield's Henry House Hill, Jackson's troops remained in place while other Southern units were falling back around them. Seeing this, Gen. Barnard Bee shouted to his troops, "There stands Jackson like a stone wall. Rally around the Virginians." Jackson's resolve and that of his troops stemmed the Confederate retreat and helped to win the battle for the South.

General Jackson and his staff at prayer in camp.
A devout Presbyterian, Jackson believed that he was on a divine mission and avoided fighting on the Sabbath.

After First Bull Run, Jackson was promoted to major general and placed in charge of the Confederate troops in Virginia's Shenandoah Valley. There, in spring 1862, he emerged as a bold, innovative strategist. Following his dictum to "always mystify, mislead, and surprise the enemy," Jackson led his force of 17,000 on a 440-mile march up and down the Shenandoah Valley, baffling the Union commanders and defeating three Federal armies totaling more than twice his number. Stonewall's "foot cavalry"—as his hard-marching soldiers called themselves—initially thought he was crazy, but as the effect of Jackson's brilliantly planned battles against the Yankees became evident, they quickly gave him their loyalty and respect.

Immediately following his victory in the Shenandoah, in June 1862, Jackson was ordered to Richmond to assist Robert E. Lee in driving the Federal troops from the outskirts of the Confederate capital. However, it took a six-week march through the valley for

Jackson and his men to link up with Lee, and by the time they did so they were too exhausted to take much part in the Seven Days' Battles that pushed the Northern Army away from Richmond. The general himself was so tired that at one point he fell asleep at supper with a cracker still clenched in his mouth!

Jackson and his foot cavalry quickly redeemed themselves during Lee's August campaign, which culminated in the Second Battle of Bull Run. After defeating a portion of Gen. John Pope's Union forces at Cedar Mountain, Virginia, early in the month, Stonewall's troops marched 50 miles around the rest of Pope's army to Manassas Junction, where they lured Pope into a decisive defeat on August 29 and 30. This opened the door for Lee's invasion of Maryland in September, culminating on the 17th in the Battle of

ON THIS SPOT
FELL
MORTALLY WOUNDED
THOMAS J. JACKSON
Lt. Gen. C. S. A.
MAY 2ND 1863.

This monument on the Chancellorsville battlefield marks the spot where Stonewall Jackson was accidentally shot by his own men on the night of May 2, 1863. **He died eight days later.**

Antietam. There, in the bloodiest single day of fighting in the war, Jackson's troops played a pivotal role in holding the northern end of the Confederate line at the battlefield's Cornfield and West Woods. Afterward, Jackson was promoted to lieutenant general and given command of the 2nd Corps of Lee's Army of Northern Virginia.

Perhaps Jackson's most daring assault was his last one, at the Battle of Chancellorsville, on May 2, 1863. Facing a Federal Army of 70,000, the general led his 28,000 men on a flanking march around the Yankees, attacking them where they least expected it and routing an entire wing of the Union forces. That evening, while making a reconnaissance ride, Jackson was tragically shot by some of his own men. Following the amputation of his left arm, complications set in and the legendary Stonewall Jackson died of pneumonia at Guinea Station, Virginia, on May 10, 1863. His last words were characteristically spiritual: "Let us cross over the river and rest under the shade of the trees."

After a state funeral in Richmond, he was buried at Lexington, near his beloved Virginia Military Institute. Jackson was survived by his second wife, Anna Morrison Jackson, and a baby daughter, Julia.

MAJOR GENERAL
Lafayette McLaws *1821 – 1897*

Lafayette McLaws was one of the most dependable division commanders in the Confederate Army. Although not one of the war's brilliant strategists or most colorful figures, he was a tough fighter whose record has earned him a place among the heroes of the Lost Cause.

McLaws was born in Augusta, Georgia, on January 15, 1821. After attending the University of Virginia for a year, he was admitted to West Point in 1838, graduating near the bottom of his class in 1842. Commissioned a lieutenant in the infantry, he served at posts in the Indian Territory and the Southern states until the outbreak of the Mexican War in 1846. Assigned to the command of his wife's uncle, Gen. Zachary Taylor, McLaws saw combat at Monterey and Vera Cruz. After the war, he remained in the West, serving in New Mexico Territory and California.

Lafayette resigned from the U.S. Army on March 23, 1861, to support his native state. After making his way cross-country, McLaws was commissioned colonel of the 10th Georgia Infantry on June 17. Three months later, on September 25, he was promoted to brigadier general and given command of a brigade on the Virginia Peninsula.

During Gen. George B. McClellan's Peninsular campaign the following spring. McLaws's troops played a decisive part in holding back the Army of the Potomac at Yorktown, earning him another promotion to major general on May 23. He was subsequently assigned a division under Gen. James Longstreet, which he led with distinction throughout the Seven Days' Battles in June.

During the Antietam campaign in September, General McLaws was detailed to assist Stonewall Jackson's assault on Harpers Ferry. After the Federal garrison there surrendered on September 15, Lafayette quickly marched his troops to Sharpsburg, Maryland, to take part in the Battle of Antietam. He arrived on the field on the morning of September 17 just as Federal troops under Gen. John Sedgwick were breaking through the Confederate lines at West Wood. McLaws immediately unleashed a withering round of fire on Sedgwick's Yankees, driving the Northerners back with 2,200 casualties and saving the position for the South.

At the Battle of Fredericksburg on December 13, Lafayette's soldiers anchored the Confederate line on Marye's Heights. Protected behind a stone wall, they fought back numerous Federal assaults against the position, mowing down over 6,000 Yankee soldiers in one of the bloodiest actions of the war.

Following Fredericksburg, Lafayette's troops anchored the Confederate right at the Battle of Chancellorsville in May 1864, helping to drive the Yankees from the town after

Gruff Georgian Lafayette McLaws, one of Gen. James Longstreet's finest officers.

The infamous stone wall at Fredericksburg, behind which McLaws's troops stopped the Union assault on Marye's Heights. **It was one of the costliest actions of the war.**

Stonewall Jackson's brilliant flanking march. McLaws next distinguished himself at the Battle of Gettysburg. During Longstreet's attack on the Federal left on July 2, Lafayette led the assault against the Peach Orchard and Devil's Den, forcing the Yankees from those positions in four hours of heavy fighting.

After Gettysburg, McLaws followed Longstreet's command into Tennessee to reinforce Gen. Braxton Bragg. While he arrived too late to participate in the Battle of Chickamauga in September, he was in time to join in the subsequent Knoxville cam-

paign—much to his regret. When he failed to capture a near-impregnable Union fortification outside Knoxville on November 29, he was blamed by General Longstreet for the poorly conceived assault, even though he had proceeded according to Longstreet's plan. Relieved of his command on December 17, he was subsequently court-martialed, but all charges were dismissed by President Davis on May 7, 1864. Following this low point, McLaws was assigned to the defenses of Savannah, Georgia, where he did all he could to stem Gen. William T. Sherman's march through eastern Georgia and the Carolinas. Having neither the manpower nor the resources to halt the Yankees' advance, he finally surrendered on April 26, 1865, as part of Gen. Joseph E. Johnston's command, at Greensboro, North Carolina.

Following the surrender Lafayette McLaws settled in Savannah and entered into the insurance business, later serving as collector of internal revenue and postmaster. McLaws died in Savannah on July 24, 1897.

Index

Photo Credits